Past Masters
General Editor Keith Thomas

Carlyle

WITHDRAWN

A. L. Le Quesne

# CARLYLE

Oxford   New York

OXFORD UNIVERSITY PRESS

Oxford University Press, Walton Street, Oxford OX2 6DP

London Glasgow New York Toronto
Delhi Bombay Calcutta Madras Karachi
Kuala Lumpur Singapore Hong Kong Tokyo
Nairobi Dar es Salaam Cape Town
Melbourne Auckland

and associate companies in
Beirut Berlin Ibadan Mexico City

First published 1982 as an Oxford University Press paperback
and simultaneously in a hardback edition
Hardback reprinted 1983

British Library Cataloguing in Publication Data

Le Quesne, A.L.
Carlyle. – (Past masters)
1. Carlyle, Thomas – Criticism and interpretation
I. Title  II. Series
828'.808  PR4434
ISBN 0-19-287563-9
ISBN 0-19-287562-0 Pbk

Set by Datamove Ltd.
Printed in Great Britain at
the University Press, Oxford
by Eric Buckley
Printer to the University

# Preface

This book, I hope, speaks for itself sufficiently clearly for a formal preface to be unnecessary; but there are some debts to be acknowledged. I am grateful to Henry Hardy for inviting me to contribute to this series, to Keith Thomas for his readiness to buy a pig in a poke, and to both of them for allowing themselves to be persuaded that Carlyle is indeed the Past Master that I believe him to be. I am grateful also to the Governors of Shrewsbury School for allowing me not only a sabbatical term but the additional leave required for the completion of this book. But most of all I am indebted to the Governing Body of Christ Church for their election of me to a schoolmaster studentship, without which the essential reading on which the book is based could hardly have been undertaken; and for the friendship and hospitality which they, and the other members of Christ Church Senior Common Room, showed me while I was there. It is to them that this book is dedicated.

*Shrewsbury*                                                    A. L. Le Quesne
*5 March 1981*

# Contents

# Abbreviations

References in the text to quotations from Carlyle are given by an abbreviation of the title (sometimes with the addition of a volume number) and a page number. Except where otherwise noted below, the reference is to the most generally available collected edition of Carlyle's works, the Centenary Edition of 1896–9. I use the following abbreviations:

A     *Letters of Thomas Carlyle to his Brother Alexander*, ed. E. W. Marrs (Cambridge, Mass., 1968)

C     *Chartism*

D     *Latter-Day Pamphlets*

E     *Critical and Miscellaneous Essays*

FF     J. A. Froude, *Thomas Carlyle: A History of the First Forty Years of His Life* (London, 1882)

FL     J. A. Froude, *Thomas Carlyle: A History of his Life in London* (London, 1884)

J     *Life of John Sterling*

L     *Letters and Speeches of Oliver Cromwell*

N     *New Letters of Thomas Carlyle*, ed. A. Carlyle (London, 1904)

P     *Past and Present*

R     *The French Revolution*

S     *Sartor Resartus*

T     *Collected Letters of Thomas and Jane Welsh Carlyle*, ed. C. R. Sanders and K. J. Fielding (Durham, North Carolina, 1970– )

W     D. A. Wilson, *Carlyle Till Marriage* (London, 1923)

There are three quotations from authors other than Carlyle which, following the style of the series, are not referenced in the text. For the sake of completeness I give the references here.

The quotations from Emerson on pp. 59 and 77 are to be found in *The Correspondence of Emerson and Carlyle*, ed. J. Slater (New York, 1964), pp. 36 and 38; and George Eliot's judgement on p. 93 in *Carlyle and his Contemporaries: Essays in Honor of Charles Richard Sanders*, ed. John Clubbe (Durham, North Carolina, 1976), p. 182.

# 1 Early years

Thomas Carlyle was born on 4 December 1795 in the small market town of Ecclefechan in the Scottish county of Dumfriesshire, not far from the north shore of the Solway Firth – the eldest of James Carlyle's second family of nine children. James Carlyle was a skilled stonemason, but Dumfriesshire was a farming community, and all its trades were more or less closely related to the land. Both James Carlyle and his second wife, Margaret, were the children of farmers, and in the hard times after the end of the Napoleonic Wars he went back to farming, a trade in which two of his younger sons were to follow him. In 1827 the Carlyles finally settled at the farm of Scotsbrig – a few miles from Ecclefechan, in the same district of Annandale – where James and Margaret lived till they died, in 1832 and 1853 respectively. The roots of the Carlyles in the soil of Annandale were deep and tenacious. Thomas was to spend more than half his life in the literary world of London, but never saw himself as anything but an exile there. Up to the last years of his life he visited Annandale frequently, and its landscape came to be burdened for him with an almost overwhelming weight of associations of childhood, of bereavement, and of home. It was wholly in keeping that he chose to be buried beside the graves of his parents in Ecclefechan churchyard.

This brief account of his background already reveals three major influences on Carlyle's life. He was a Scot, a working man's son, and a man with a profound sense of family piety. His relations with his mother and with two of his younger brothers, Alexander and John, were particularly close and affectionate, as the voluminous correspondence between them testifies. The rock-like stability of his family, to which he returned for strength and refreshment throughout his life, was one of the chief formative influences upon his character, balancing an unstable and nerve-ridden temperament, prone to bouts of melancholia and prey to a chronic dyspepsia of which he was a

lifelong and anything but uncomplaining victim. His national
and social origin had a different influence on his career. Both,
especially the latter, contributed to making him a maverick and
an outsider in the English literary world, in which he became
one of the most renowned figures by the middle of the century –
a role of which both he and his public were highly conscious,
and one which he exploited with brilliant success in becoming
the leading prophetic figure of his age, the Jeremiah of nineteenth-century Britain.

Equally important for Carlyle's development was the religious
background of his youth. His family were members of the Bur-
gher Secession Church, one of the numerous splinter groups
that had rebelled against the laxity of the established Church of
Scotland in the course of the eighteenth century, and both his
childhood and his whole personality were coloured by the sternly disciplined piety of Scottish Calvinism, a tradition which he
outgrew intellectually but never spiritually. All his later references to his religious upbringing are nostalgic: the unquestioning faith of his parents' generation came to be for him one of
the hallmarks of the healthy condition of a man or a society,
and the absence of faith in Victorian Britain only reinforced the
vehemence of his insistence on the need for it.

James Carlyle was a figure of formidable authority. His whole
life was based on an unbending ethic of hard work and auster-
ity, an ethic which harmonised readily with the teachings of his
Church. His children inherited these values from him, Thomas
perhaps more than any: he never found it easy to communicate
with his father, though the devotion he felt to his memory and
example came out most poignantly in the memoir that he wrote
after James Carlyle's death in 1832, which was later published
in his *Reminiscences*. The circumstances of the family were always straitened, although never poverty-stricken. In England at
this time a child from such a background could hardly have
aspired to any education that took him beyond the three Rs.
But Scotland was peculiar in its tradition of popular education
reaching back to the Reformation. Carlyle went not merely to
the village school at Ecclefechan, but on to the neighbouring
grammar school at Annan, and thence to Edinburgh University
in 1809, at the (not in fact unusually young) age of thirteen.

Like many other poor men's sons, he walked there – a distance, in his case, of nearly a hundred miles. He found his own lodgings, sent his washing back to Ecclefechan by the local carrier, and received in return a supply of oatmeal which formed the main item of his diet.

Edinburgh, like the other Scottish universities, but unlike the English ones of the time, saw it as its primary teaching function to provide a basic general education, at approximately what we would now regard as secondary level, for a body of unprivileged and often very poor students, most of whom would then hope to go on to careers in the Church, the law, medicine or, at worst, teaching. This education was not free, but it was very cheap – two to three guineas a year. It is hardly surprising that students received little in return for this beyond the right to attend lectures and to use the library. The curriculum was perceptibly wider than those of Oxford and Cambridge – Carlyle attended courses in natural philosophy (in effect, physical science) as well as Latin, Greek, logic and mathematics – but not very demanding in its standards. Although Carlyle in later life could read both Latin and Greek with appreciation, he never possessed the easy fluency in them with which his ablest contemporaries in England emerged from Oxford and Cambridge.

If Carlyle had not been recognised early as a boy of unusual promise, it is very unlikely that he would have got to university at all, for low though the fees were, they were still a heavy burden on a household like James Carlyle's. Only one of his three younger brothers was to follow him to university – the other two remained on the farm. His parents' hope, like that of many similar poor families with one able son at the university, was that he would go into the ministry of his Church, and it was toward this end that his studies at Edinburgh were directed. Like many other students similarly situated, he did not take a degree, but instead, when his four years' course at Edinburgh ended in 1813, went on to a further part-time course in divinity, designed to enable him to earn his living during the day and to study in the evenings. This course would have taken seven years to complete. For a poor student like Carlyle, the natural recourse for a living in the interim was to schoolteaching, and Carlyle accordingly became a teacher, at first at his own old school in Annan, later at Kirkcaldy in Fife. But rebellion had been rising in him for years, and he hated teaching. Finally he took two decisive steps: in 1817 he abandoned all ideas of the Church as a career, and in 1818 he resigned from his post at Kirkcaldy.

To understand this change of course, it is necessary to understand the impact that Edinburgh had had upon him. The world of early nineteenth-century Edinburgh was immensely wider and more sophisticated than the Annandale of Carlyle's childhood, and the education that it had to offer had in it the stiffening backbone of a systematic philosophy that exposed the inherited values of Carlyle's childhood to strenuous challenge. Edinburgh had been the citadel of the eighteenth-century Scottish Enlightenment. The European Enlightenment had struck deeper root in Scotland, and thrown up a more vigorous crop of native thinkers – Hume in philosophy, Adam Smith in economics, Robertson in history – than anywhere else in Britain. The values they advocated were the characteristic values of the Enlightenment – empiricism in philosophy, scepticism toward all revealed religion, a primarily utilitarian account of morals, a coolly objective rationalism that queried tradition, deprecated emotion and enthusiasm, and in seeking explanations of the world about it required above all that they should be compatible with common sense and observed facts. As Carlyle was later to write in *Sartor Resartus*, in satirical retrospect on his student days at Edinburgh,

> We boasted ourselves a Rational University; in the highest degree hostile to Mysticism; thus was the young vacant mind furnished with much talk about Progress of the Species, Dark Ages, Prejudice, and the like; so that all were quickly enough blown out into a state of windy argumentativeness; whereby the better sort had soon to end in sick, impotent Scepticism; the worser sort explode in finished Self-conceit, and to all spiritual intents become dead. (S 90)

No doubt there were plenty of Carlyle's contemporaries in Edinburgh who passed placidly through the university without ever noticing the values it stood for – as is true of all universities at all times – or at least without ever troubling their heads about them. This option was not available to Carlyle. He had an acutely receptive and sensitive mind, which reacted immediately and sharply to the intellectual environment, and from the first he had an avid thirst for knowledge, reading insatiably now that for the first time he found a good library at his disposal. Poverty, a pride in his extraordinary ability, and a formidable capacity for sarcasm (these last two were to be strongly marked features of his character all his life) made him something of a solitary among his fellows, and further intensified his inner life and conflicts. He could not but be aware of the crucial challenge posed by the intellectual assumptions of his Edinburgh world to the values of his Annandale upbringing, its piety, its other-worldliness, its unquestioning religious faith.

This challenge, and Carlyle's response to it, can be seen as the central feature of his entire intellectual and moral life. The conflict took a form which, in similar cases, is familiar enough. The immediate impact of Edinburgh University and all it stood for on the thirteen-year old boy was overwhelming. The religious faith in which he had been brought up disintegrated before the challenge of the newer and, it seemed, more sophisticated creed. Carlyle himself told the story of how at the age of fourteen he shocked his mother by enquiring sceptically, 'Did God Almighty come down and make wheelbarrows in a shop?' (W 78). The disintegration was gradual, but it was final. Carlyle was never to regain the faith of his childhood, and it is this that explains his eventual decision, in 1817, to abandon the idea of entering the ministry. But while destroying his faith in the creed in which he had been brought up, the new creed never succeeded in making a true convert of Carlyle; what it did was to create in him an agonising sense of alienation and desolation. A sense of betrayal towards his parents was clearly one factor in this, but only a minor one: the central factor was that he was a man for whom a religious creed and a sense of transcendental purpose were in the strictest sense of the word vital. It was Miguel de Unamuno, a Spanish admirer of Carlyle in this century, who said, 'It is not rational necessity, but vital anguish that impels us to believe in God'; but the words might very well have been Carlyle's own.

The immediate aftermath of Carlyle's university years was,

therefore, a decade of intense intellectual and moral conflict, as he attempted to find some way of reconciling his desperate spiritual needs with what seemed to be the irresistible demands of intellectual integrity. But before we go further into this period, there are two final points which need to be made about his university years. One is that the Edinburgh of Carlyle's youth was in its silver, not its golden, age; the intellectual fires which had glowed so bright there in the eighteenth century were dying down. Most of the very great men were dead; arguably the last of them, the moral philosopher Dugald Stewart, retired from his chair in 1810, the year after Carlyle's arrival, and by the standards of the great the men who taught Carlyle were second-rate. Did Carlyle's inability to find satisfaction in the intellectual tradition of the Scottish Enlightenment owe something to the fact that that tradition was already on the decline, already too far worked out to have enough to offer a student of outstanding ability?

The second, very striking point is that the parts of the syllabus which made the strongest appeal to Carlyle at the time were mathematics and the natural sciences, and he seems to have had outstanding abilities in these fields. They were recognised by the professor of mathematics, Leslie, and were sufficient for him to be a credible candidate for the chair of mathematics at Sandhurst in 1822, and a somewhat less credible one for the chair of astronomy at St Andrew's in 1834. His later career followed so different a course that it could almost be taken as a case study supporting his own frequently expressed belief that genius is non-specific, and can be turned to any use. Clearly this early taste for mathematics and science is hard to discern in his public writings, some of which might well have benefited from a larger infusion of these disciplines. It is relevant, though, that it seems above all to have been the pure logic of mathematics, especially geometry, rather than the empiricism of the physical sciences, that appealed to him; and it is fair to add that even in the last years of Carlyle's life his friend John Tyndall, the great physicist, bore witness to his remarkable ability to grasp scientific concepts.

After throwing up his post at Kirkcaldy in 1818, Carlyle withdrew into an inner wilderness from which he emerged only gradually in the course of the 1820s. Economically, morally and intellectually the early years after 1818 in particular were a period of agonising disorientation and instability, a crisis which was reflected by a partial breakdown in health, in the form of a chronic and crippling dyspepsia from which he was never afterwards wholly free, and an increasingly morbid sensitivity to noise which also never left him. Carlyle was endowed with a nervous system of pathological sensitivity. This was, no doubt, the reverse side of the brilliant powers of description and total recall that make his letters and his *Reminiscences* such vivid documents. But at this time almost every letter is punctuated with complaints of nights rendered sleepless by street and house noises, and of days made unproductive by agonies of indigestion; and, equally typically, with expressions of furious determination to overcome these afflictions, the sense of Puritan purpose working through. He did not know in what direction his life was going or how he should earn a living, and he was appalled by the prospect of a world which seemed now to have lost its spiritual dimension. In words which he later put into the mouth of Teufelsdrockh, the central figure of *Sartor Resartus*:

> To me the Universe was all void of Life, of Purpose, of Volition, even of Hostility: it was one huge, dead, immeasurable Steam-engine, rolling on, in its dead indifference, to grind me limb from limb. O, the vast, gloomy, solitary Golgotha, and Mill of Death! Why was the Living banished thither companionless, conscious? (S 133)

Amid this desolation, the one point of security and comfort that remained was the unswerving support of his family. In Annandale, in the simple farm-house in which by now the family was living, he was always sure of love and acceptance. Without the continual flow of their gifts of farm produce it is difficult to see how in these years he could have survived at all in Edinburgh, where for most of the time he eked out a life in cheap lodgings. He toyed with the idea of a career in law, only to throw it up as he rapidly discovered that he had no taste for it. He made a little money in odd tutoring jobs, most of which he disliked, and a little more by writing articles for an encyclopaedia – important as his first published writings, but otherwise the merest journalistic hackwork. But he continued to read omnivorously, accumulating the vast arsenal of literary knowledge and reference which he was later to put to splendid use in his mature writing. He also did two other extremely important things. In 1819 or thereabouts he learned German; and in 1821 he met Jane Welsh. These two encounters were to do much to shape the rest of his life.

Carlyle was a more than competent linguist. He already knew French, Latin and Greek, and was later to acquire Italian, Spanish and Danish. But German was to him far more than a language; it was the revelation of a new attitude to life which held out the prospect of a solution to the torments of intellectual scepticism and spiritual emptiness. And indeed in 1819 German was a very exciting language for an Englishman to learn, since it gave him access to a literary and philosophical renaissance that was still, unlike the tradition of the Enlightenment, in its most vital and creative phase, and still ranks as one of the major milestones of modern European intellectual history. This German Renaissance was itself part of the broader European movement of Romanticism, which in the last third of the eighteenth century was felt to different degrees throughout Western Europe. In the names of instinct, emotion, introspection, tradition, history, the nation, it everywhere mounted a challenge to the values of the Enlightenment: reason, scepticism, universalism, objectivity, the appeal to first principles. To the castaways of the Enlightenment, like Carlyle or, later, John Stuart Mill, it came like the discovery of a spring of fresh water at the moment of death from thirst. Romanticism had struck vigorous root in England too, most notably in the school of the Lake Poets, Coleridge, Wordsworth and Southey; and it is worth asking why Carlyle could not have found his salvation nearer home in them, and why he had to go to Germany for it. But such questions can never be fully answered. Carlyle's poetic sensibilities were always cramped and narrow, certainly. The Lake Poets may have been simply too much figures of the literary and political establishment by the time Carlyle entered upon his years of travail to hold any attraction for him. But very probably the main explanation is that the German Renaissance was a much broader and more imposing intellectual phe-

nomenon than English Romanticism was ever to become. It had
not merely a new poetry to its credit, but a new drama and a
new philosophy as well; it had in Kant (arguably also in Hegel)
one of the seminal figures in the history of European philosophy, and in Goethe a writer whose breadth of genius has often
prompted comparisons with Dante and Shakespeare.

In the decade after 1819 Carlyle read voluminously in German literature, and his indebtedness to the German writers of
the last generation was manifold – to Goethe above all. He grap-
pled vigorously with the work of the philosophers, Kant,
Fichte, Schelling and Schlegel, for he recognised that the Enlightenment was principally a philosophical phenomenon, and must
be met with its own weapons on its own ground. But Carlyle was
never by nature a philosopher, and although he satisfied himself
that in Kant and Fichte he had discovered the answer to what
was to him the desolating rationalism of the eighteenth century,
what he in fact got from them seems to have been limited for
the most part to ideas and phrases taken out of context and
frequently misunderstood. It was the imaginative writers of the
German Renaissance who spoke most strongly to him and who
helped him most in his time of greatest need, and among them
especially the dramatist Schiller, the humorist and satirist Jean
Paul Richter, and of course Goethe – or more correctly,
perhaps, some of Goethe: *Faust* to a limited extent, and some of
the later works, but especially *Wilhelm Meister*, whose theme of
a young man finding his way through intellectual and spiritual
perplexities to self-fulfilment had an obvious relevance to his
own condition.

For the rest of Carlyle's life, Germany was to stand to him as
the exemplar of a healthy society (a view perhaps made easier
by the fact that he first visited it in 1852 at the age of fifty-six).
For twenty years at least, Goethe (with whom he came to cor-
respond on terms of close discipleship) was to be his spiritual
lodestar, the incarnate proof that intellectual integrity and faith
could still be reconciled. Carlyle saw in him the teacher of a
sternly stoical morality whose watchword was *Entsagen*, renunciation; and, not least, the model of the man of letters as an
intermediary between the two worlds of the Ideal and the Real,
the Divine and the Human.

In all this there was a good deal of misunderstanding and distortion; but this is of secondary importance. Whether Carlyle misread his German mentors or not, there is no question of the importance of what he *thought* he learned from them, or of its effect on his life. What he emerged with was a fluctuating, sometimes inconsistent intellectual amalgam, deriving from the Puritanism of his family background and the impact of the ideas of the Enlightenment as well as from the German intellectual renaissance; and it was perhaps only because the German influence was the most recent that he saw it as dominant. But in a mind as powerful as Carlyle's the amalgam, however mongrel its origins and imprecise its intellectual formulations, became something highly original and of compelling force – above all imaginative force – to the generation to which he proclaimed it. What were its main elements?

Carlyle commonly described the central feature either as 'Mysticism' or as 'Natural Supernaturalism'; the latter description seems to come nearer to his meaning, with its implication of a universe of two separate, but intimately related, orders, but the former has the advantage of making clear Carlyle's primary emphasis upon the supernatural order. More than anything, Carlyle's encounter with the German Renaissance restored his faith in the existence of a transcendent spiritual order which underlay the apparent world and gave it whatever reality it might possess. Throughout the middle period of Carlyle's life, nothing is more typical of him than the quality of stereoscopic vision, his habit of translating this world in terms of values derived from a different and invisible one. This characteristic could obviously be traced to the religious beliefs of his childhood, but rested more immediately on the philosophic idealism of his German mentors – and, one is bound to add, it had in him all the force of a genuinely native vision. A passage from his journal in 1835 is typical:

The world looks often quite spectral to me; sometimes, as in Regent Street the other night (my nerves being all shattered), quite hideous, discordant, almost infernal. I had been at Mrs Austin's, heard Sydney Smith for the first time guffawing,

other persons prating, jargoning. *To me through these thin cob-
webs Death and Eternity sate glaring.* (FL I 54, my italics)

'To me', one notes. Implicit in his vision was the realisation
that the rest of the world, with the rarest exceptions, did not
share it; and with it a sense of separateness and what can only
be called a consciousness of mission. Carlyle rationalised this
'double vision' in terms of the distinction, also German, between 'Reason' and 'Understanding', which he derived from
Kant, possibly via Coleridge: Understanding, the calculating
capacity which deals with the quantifiable world, with what can
be weighed and measured; and the confusingly-named 'Reason',
the profounder capacity for insight into the real nature of things
and the world of values. But as often with Carlyle, the rationa-
lisation was less important than the experience: the experience
of seeing in two dimensions where most people saw only in one.
This one-dimensional vision was, to Carlyle, the myopia which
the world had contracted from the one-eyed philosophers of the
Enlightenment, and to which the transcendentalism of the Germans was the antidote. From another German, Fichte, he derived the idea of the man of letters as the prophet of this transcendent order, whose mission it was to make men aware of that
order and of its demands upon them. Goethe was to him the
supreme example of how that mission might be performed; and
inevitably he came to see himself as sharing the same calling.
'Doubtful it is in the highest degree', he wrote about 1830,
'whether ever I shall make men hear my voice to any purpose or
not. Certain only, that I shall be a *failure* if I do not' (FF II 81).

There is a danger that all this may sound very abstract, as
indeed, in its philosophical origins, it no doubt is. But Carlyle's
gift for metaphysics was limited, and his mind was intensely
concrete. His rediscovery of what I have called the transcendent
order of things, and his insistence that it alone was the source of
all reality and of all true value, was combined with an emphatic
insistence that it was only through its reflections in this world
that it could be discerned, and only by activity in this world –
by practical work – that its demands could be met. It is here, no
doubt, that the influence of his childhood Puritanism shows

most clearly through the German surface. Life to Carlyle was intensely earnest – 'Ernst ist das Leben' was one of the quotations from Goethe that was most frequently on his lips; dilettantism was one of the mortal sins. The supreme justification of a man's life was honest work, solidly performed. In the stout masonry of a bridge that his father had built he saw the symbol of a life properly lived. For all his harsh criticism of the self-seeking materialism of the industrialists of the early Industrial Revolution, the disciples of Mammon, they were preferable in his eyes to the landed aristocracy because they worked, they *did* something: asked to justify their existence, they could at least point to Manchester and to uncountable millions of cotton shirts, where the landed aristocrat could point to nothing but a row of dead partridges.

In the early 1820s Carlyle began by degrees to work himself out of the pit of depression and ill health into which he had fallen, and to make out with more certainty the path that lay before him. In retrospect, he himself came to lay particular stress upon a moment of illumination, akin to a religious conversion, that came upon him in Edinburgh in the summer of 1821 or 1822, as the crux of his recovery. In fact, the process seems to have been more gradual; but its reality is not in doubt. Although the ravages of dyspepsia and an excessively sensitive nervous system haunted him throughout his life, at least the intellectual and spiritual agonies were triumphantly overcome; he knew what he believed, and never thereafter doubted it. The discovery of German literature was not the only factor in this recovery, but it was a crucial one. His widening range of personal friendships was also important. Loneliness is one of the penalties of genius, and, given the humbleness of Carlyle's social background, it is not surprising that for years he had to find his friends among his intellectual inferiors – an experience that undoubtedly reinforced the tendencies to pride and contempt which had been apparent since his youth. But in the world of Edinburgh he began to make contact with men who could match him intellectually, and who on their side could recognise in him a young man with capacities far above the ordinary.

By near unanimous testimony, Carlyle was an extremely impressive person: a tall, raw-boned figure of compressed and formidable strength of character, of complete spontaneity, of great originality, and of brilliant and vivid powers of self-expression. As these powers began to approach their full unfolding in the 1820s, recognition of his genius grew. It was greatly aided by the friendship of his Annandale compatriot Edward Irving, who had known Carlyle throughout his blackest years. Irving was a few years Carlyle's senior, and himself a man of considerable intellectual attainment; he sensed the quality of Carlyle's mind very early, and gave him warm, generous help and encouragement throughout his years of depression. In the early 1820s Irving was starting on the meteoric career in the Church which was to lead him to brief fame and public sensation as a millennialist preacher in London, soon and tragically succeeded by ostracism, mockery and an early death. It was through him that in 1822 Carlyle was introduced to a distinguished Anglo-Indian family, the Bullers, and became tutor to their two sons. This tutorship lasted two years, and marks an important turning-point in Carlyle's career. He was proud, touchy, morbidly sensitive, and very difficult; but the Bullers had the insight to see through this and to recognise his exceptional qualities. They treated him with great consideration, and the two boys became devoted to him, especially the elder, Charles Buller, himself destined for a brief but distinguished career in politics. The Bullers gave Carlyle his first entrée to upper-class English society; they were also responsible for his first visit to London (in 1824) and his first visit to the Continent, a week spent with them in Paris. For all this, Irving was responsible; but he was also responsible for the far more fateful introduction of Carlyle to Jane Welsh.

Jane Welsh was the daughter of a prosperous doctor in Haddington, a country town outside Edinburgh. Irving had been her tutor, and there seems little doubt that they had been in love with each other; but Irving was already pledged to another woman. He introduced Carlyle to the Welsh household in 1821, and it was not long before Carlyle too fell in love with her. By all accounts she must have been enchantingly attractive, if not beautiful, with brilliant qualities of mind – witty, pert, vivacious, mercurial and elusive. She had a passion for education and self-improvement, and sensed at once that in Carlyle she had found a man who could uniquely guide her to what she wanted; but it took him five years of hard wooing to convert this unofficial mentorship into her own and her mother's hard-won consent to their marriage. It was to be one of the most fateful and controversial literary marriages of the nineteenth century, and argument has raged over it ever since. Jane Welsh was a brilliant woman, as the distinguished circle of friends who for so many years frequented the Carlyles' 'at home' evenings in London eagerly testified. It was her misfortune that she was endowed with a nervous sensibility almost as acute as Carlyle's own, and a hypochondria that exceeded his; for the last thirty years of her life she was a martyr to headaches and insomnia. The Carlyles had no children; it was a devoted marriage, but latterly it was also for her a tormented one, and it can be, and has been, read in many ways. It can be said that for two people of such temperaments, life together could never have been easy anyway. Equally, feminists have interpreted the marriage, not altogether implausibly, as a typical example of male tyranny and female subjection. It is certainly true that Carlyle's attentions to Lady Ashburton in the 1840s and 1850s did nothing to make his wife's lot easier, harmless though they appeared in his own eyes. Froude, Carlyle's latter-day friend and biographer, hinted that Carlyle was impotent and that the marriage was never consummated, which, if true, would certainly account for its tensions; but the evidence, such as it is, seems to give him little support. It remains true that the early years of the marriage at least seem to have been idyllically happy, that the element of love on both sides remained strong and genuine, and that after Jane's death in 1866, the whole story of the remaining fifteen years of Carlyle's life goes to prove the truth of the words he put on her tombstone, that the light of his life went out with her.

By the time of their marriage in 1826, Carlyle was modestly but firmly established in the literary world of Edinburgh, and was beginning to make a name for himself further afield as a translator and critic of German literature. His first public appearance in this role was an essay on 'Faust' published in 1822, followed by a much more substantial series of articles (later republished as a book) on Schiller, and a translation of the first part of *Wilhelm Meister*. Public awareness of the significance of the German literary renaissance was just awakening in England, thanks to the spadework of earlier critics and translators and above all of Coleridge (whom Carlyle met in his old age, but to whose achievement he did a good deal less than justice). Carlyle therefore found the ground to some extent prepared, and his work had a ready market; but he nevertheless deserves a large share of the credit for transforming the attitude of the educated English public to German literature (and above all to the work of Goethe) in the second. quarter of the nineteenth century. Between 1822 and 1832 he published some twenty major essays in this field, and although he only fleetingly returned to it afterwards, it is important that it was in this intermediary, rather than creative, role that his name was first made. Editors, aware of the growing public interest in the subject, welcomed his work, and through it he became known to several of the most influential of them, including Francis Jeffrey of the *Edinburgh Review*.

The *Edinburgh*, founded in 1802, was the leading organ of liberal ideas in the country, and had set the example for a number of other 'Reviews', which by the 1820s were the most influential section of the British periodical press. The 'reviews' of which they consisted were often long essays only slimly related to the books they were supposedly reviewing. This was a literary form capable of brilliant exploitation, and in the 1820s there was no better way for a young man of literary aspirations to make himself known to the reading public than through the *Edinburgh* and its great Tory rival, the *Quarterly Review*; the most dazzling example of a reputation made in this way is Macaulay. Carlyle lacked Macaulay's advantages of a brilliant Cambridge career and a footing in the upper classes, and his literary range at this time was much narrower; but it was the Reviews, and especially the generous, though not uncritical, patronage of Jeffrey that enabled Carlyle to support himself and his wife, and gradually to acquire a literary reputation that by 1834 made a move to London feasible. The yoke of working for periodicals, and especially the necessity of subjecting his work to the varying political and literary whims and crotchets of their editors was always irksome to Carlyle, all the more so since his opinions and his style became increasingly idiosyncratic and more and more alarming to editors in the later 1820s; but he had good reason to be grateful to the Reviews, for it is hard indeed to see how else he could have built a literary career.

The first part of the Carlyles' married life was spent in Edinburgh, where their vivid personalities and the quality of their conversation swiftly made their modest house the centre of an extremely lively intellectual coterie, forerunner of their later and much more famous one in London. But Carlyle's income from his writings was both small and precarious. During the 1820s he made several abortive applications for academic posts; but although his abilities could easily have justified such an appointment, he was probably always too much of an original and too anxious for a wider audience to have fitted comfortably into the Scottish academic world. It was poverty more than anything that drove them to leave Edinburgh in 1828 and move to the very remote farmhouse of Craigenputtock in Dumfriesshire, which had been left to Jane at her father's death. Craigenputtock was within comfortable range of Carlyle's family in Annandale, and for their first two years there they had the company of Carlyle's brother Alexander, who farmed the land. They were completely isolated there from the literary world, if also from the noises and trials of urban life which bore so heavily on Carlyle's nerves. This isolation was broken only twice in six years, by prolonged visits to London in the winter of 1831–2 and to Edinburgh early in 1833, and it became increasingly unendurable as time went by. Visitors to Craigenputtock were few and far between – though they did include Jeffrey and his wife, in 1828, and in 1833 the young American Transcendentalist R. W. Emerson. Emerson had read and greatly admired Carlyle's review articles, and it was he who originated the strong and enduring tradition of American admiration of Carlyle's work.

The stream of Carlyle's thought and writing was flowing broader, deeper, and stronger with the years. The range of his articles widened, at first to British and French authors, with notable essays on Burns in 1828, on Voltaire in 1829, and on Diderot and Johnson in 1833, and then to social and historical subjects, with 'Signs of the Times' in 1829, 'On History' in 1830, 'Characteristics' in 1831 and 'Cagliostro' in 1833. In-

creasingly, he grew impatient with the limitations of review
work, feeling that he could only achieve complete self-expression
through a book of his own. He had already, in 1827, attempted
a novel (*Wotton Reinfred*), heavily autobiographical in content
and owing a good deal to *Wilhelm Meister*; but fiction never
suited his talents (or his tastes) and he soon abandoned it. The
remarkable span of Carlyle's mind made the finding of a suitable literary form, as of a suitable career, unusually difficult. In
1830 he contemplated the idea of a major historical work on
Luther, but had to abandon it since a trip to Germany was
beyond the Carlyles' means. Instead, in the autumn of 1830, he
started work on what was to become *Sartor Resartus* and over
the winter of 1831–2 he paid a visit to London in the hope of
finding a publisher for it. In this he failed, but the visit was
extremely important to him (and to Jane, who later joined him
in London) for other reasons. He was present in the capital at
one of the peaks of the Reform Bill crisis, an experience which
gave him an altogether new insight into the problems of English
society. He started to build up a richly talented group of friends
among the London intelligentsia. He became aware of the extent to which the ideas he had been propagating in his review
articles over the last decade had begun to wake an echo in some
of the liveliest minds of the new generation. He found himself
for the first time with a circle, not merely of admirers, but of
disciples, whose allegiance was the more flattering because of
their own exceptional abilities. Outstanding among them was
the young John Stuart Mill, just then experiencing a strong
emotional revulsion against the arid Utilitarianism of his upbringing. Mill hardly knew what to make of Carlyle, but he
recognised him at once as the most formidable moral and intellectual force he had yet encountered. Their friendship was
close, and until they drifted apart at the end of the 1830s it was
one of the most interesting crossroads in the development of
nineteenth-century English ideas.

The Carlyles returned to Craigenputtock in the spring of
1832, their departure from London hastened by the death of
Carlyle's father. But they were never at ease there again. The
experience of the intellectual life of London, and of the easy
contact with editors and publishers that could only be found

there, made the isolation of Craigenputtock unendurable. *Sartor* was finally accepted for publication in instalments in the newly-founded *Fraser's Magazine* in the autumn of 1833. On the strength of this, in the spring of 1834, the Carlyles made the decision to risk a move to London, in spite of the economic uncertainty it involved. In June they settled into the house in Cheyne Row, Chelsea, then a rural suburb of London, in which they were to spend the rest of their lives; and in July Carlyle started work on what was to become *The French Revolution*.

## 2 Sartor Resartus

The publication of *Sartor Resartus* in *Fraser's* contributed little to either Carlyle's purse or to his reputation, for such attention as it attracted from the magazine's readers was almost uniformly unfavourable. In England, except among the small circle of Carlyle's admirers, the waters closed over it without a trace. In so far as it found an audience at all, it was, thanks to Emerson's efforts on his friend's behalf, in America, where it was published as a book in 1836. In England it was only in 1838, after the success of *The French Revolution* had established Carlyle's name in 1837, that a similar edition appeared. *Sartor* has long since triumphed over its critics. To a modern judgement it is one of the most unquestionable works of genius written in English in the entire nineteenth century. But it remains a ruggedly difficult book to approach, and it is easy to understand the incomprehension and hostility that greeted its first appearance. In novelty of style, diction and form it posed a challenge to its readers only comparable to that posed by *Ulysses* in the twentieth century.

*Sartor Resartus* is a weird Romantic masterpiece which defies either classification or summary. It has sometimes been called a novel, but it strains even the highly elastic modern concept of that form, let alone the early nineteenth-century one. It was Carlyle's first full-scale proclamation of 'natural supernaturalism', of the newly-recovered Idealism that he had learned from Germany. This alone still sounded strange enough to most English readers in the early 1830s; but it is the form of the book that is truly extraordinary. It appears at first to be an account, by an admiring but dubious 'Editor', of a work by an outlandish German philosopher, Diogenes Teufelsdrockh ('Devil's Dung'), Professor of Things in General at the University of Weissnichtwo ('Don't Know Where'), on the 'Philosophy of Clothes'. The 'Philosophy of Clothes' turns out to be a brilliantly ingenious and amusing metaphor for Carlyle's Idealism,

clothes being the symbol of the real world which at once dis-
guises and conceals, but also reveals and expresses, the ideal
world (the 'body') beneath. The metaphor is twisted and turned
and held up to the light successively in innumerable different
ways and senses, with the breathtaking swiftness and ingenuity
of a conjuror; but, tantalisingly, we are given Teufelsdrockh's
work only in quotations and in paraphrases, interspersed with
lamentations from the 'Editor' about the outlandishness of
Teufelsdrockh's ideas and style. Half-way through, he sets
about trying to clarify these by attempting a biography of
Teufelsdrockh based on a mass of fragmentary jottings sent to
him by a friend in Weissnichtwo – a section which in part
clearly reflects Carlyle's autobiography.

All this is weird enough, but the effect is heightened by the
extraordinary style. This had been developing by degrees in
Carlyle's review essays in the later 1820s, as he acquired more
confidence in himself and a greater readiness to break with the
canons of Augustan English inherited from the eighteenth century. But it was in *Sartor* that a fully-developed 'Carlylese' first
saw the light of day; and it is small wonder that readers were
bewildered. They had to cope not only with a cast of characters including such unfamiliar figures as Herr Towgood, the
Hofrath Heuschrecke, and an Angelic Smuggler who appears at
the North Cape and tries to push Teufelsdrockh over the edge
of the cliff, but with an English prose capable of such baroque
effects as these:

> 'In the mean while, is it not beautiful to see five-million quin-
> tals of Rags picked annually from the Laystall; and annually,
> after being macerated, hot-pressed, printed-on, and sold, –
> returned thither; filling so many hungry mouths by the way?
> Thus is the Laystall, especially with its Rags or Clothes-
> rubbish, the grand Electric Battery, and Fountain-of-
> Motion, from which and to which the Social Activities (like
> vitreous and resinous Electricities) circulate, in larger or
> smaller circles, through the mighty, billowy, stormtost Chaos
> of Life, which they keep alive!' – Such passages fill us, who
> love the man, and partly esteem him, with a very mixed feel-
> ing. (S 34–5)

The Editor's qualifying reservation at the end of this passage is typical; but, though he himself usually writes in a somewhat soberer style, even he is capable of such strange apostrophes as this:

Consider, thou foolish Teufelsdrockh, what benefits unspeakable all ages and sexes derive from Clothes. For example, when thou thyself, a watery, pulpy, slobbery freshman and new-comer in this Planet, sattest muling and puking in thy nurse's arms; sucking thy coral, and looking forth into the world in the blankest manner, what hadst thou been without thy blankets, and bibs, and other nameless hulls? A terror to thyself and mankind! (S 45)

The origins of this rambling, turbulent, ejaculatory, vastly self-indulgent and metaphorical style have been much discussed. Rabelais, Sterne and Jean Paul Richter are the models most often mentioned, and the Germanisms, such as the regular use of the second person singular and the employment of capitals at the beginning of words, are obvious. Carlyle always insisted that the style was not artificial but natural, and derived from the pithy and vehement speech of his elders, especially his father, in Annandale; but this can only be true of its remoter origins. There has likewise been great debate as to whether it is one of the best or one of the worst styles in English, and on this no agreement is possible. What can be said is that, for better or worse, the style is unmistakable, and satisfies to a remarkable degree Carlyle's own criterion for style, that it should fit its author like a skin. This is style in its extreme Romantic form, designed to conform to no established canons, but seen purely as a medium of self-expression. Few would deny that it is capable of moments of great beauty – as in a familiar passage from *Oliver Cromwell* describing the night before the battle of Dunbar:

And so the soldiers stand to their arms, or lie within instant reach of their arms, all night; being upon an engagement very difficult indeed. The night is wild and wet; – 2nd of September means 12th by our calendar: the Harvest Moon wades

deep among clouds of sleet and hail. Whoever has a heart for
prayer, let him pray now, for the wrestle of death is at hand.
Pray, – and withal keep his powder dry! And be ready for
extremities, and quit himself like a man! – Thus they pass
the night; making that Dunbar Peninsula and Brock Rivulet
long memorable to me. We English have some tents; the
Scots have none. The hoarse sea moans bodeful, swinging
low and heavy against these whinstone bays; the sea and the
tempests are abroad, all else asleep but we, – and there is One
that rides on the wings of the wind. (L II 205)

But whatever is to be said about Carlyle's style, it was un-
questionably not likely to win easy acceptance from the public.
The same was true of *Sartor*'s baffling and elusive form. More
than a century after it was written, it is possible to see it in
context and to realise that Carlyle is looking back mockingly on
his own past as a review writer, from which *Sartor* marks a
decisive departure, and in doing so making brilliant imaginative use of the conventions of the review. Even Teufelsdrockh's
biography, in Book II, reflects the form which Carlyle had
evolved for his major review articles of the late 1820s; this was a
combination of a life-history of the writer with an analysis of his
writings, the two being inseparable to Carlyle – the essays on
Burns and Johnson are excellent examples. *Sartor* is a fictitious
review article in which, bafflingly, the author identifies with the
reviewed rather than the reviewer. The 'Editor' becomes the
voice of the doubting British public, or of the best-inclined portion of it; in so far as Carlyle's voice is heard in the book at all,
it is in the words of Teufelsdrockh. The devices by which Carlyle conceals his own position and identity in the book are,
among other things, the stratagem of a proud man discounting
in advance the incomprehension and the hostility which he anticipated in his readers. But these devices create a strange sense
of receding identities which remarkably anticipates some typical
forms of twentieth-century consciousness; and they clearly had
enduring significance for Carlyle, for throughout his later writings he continued to use the device of inventing imaginary,
usually German, professors as mouth-pieces for some of his own
rhapsodical and high-flown utterances.

The formal and stylistic originality of *Sartor* are thus not in doubt. The content is another matter. *Sartor* is important because it represents the first connected setting-out of the thematic ideas that run through and dominate all Carlyle's later work. In it, as he himself says of Teufelsdrockh, 'his character has now taken its ultimate bent, and no new revolution, of importance, is to be looked for' (S 162). With one major reservation, which we shall come to, he appraised his own future intellectual development to a nicety in these words. The relative emphasis he laid on the various themes was to shift considerably; but the themes themselves are all there in *Sartor*. There is the central point of the 'Philosophy of Clothes', the Idealism that he had learned from his German reading: the idea that the material order of things represents only a projection, or, to use Carlyle's own term, a 'bodying-forth', of a spiritual order, the only ultimate reality, which underlies it. The material order is limited by time and space, but these are themselves illusions, concealing the realities of Eternity and Infinity. Man is essentially a spiritual being, and his affinity is with the spiritual order; but the spiritual can only be approached through the material, and man's function in this world is to bring the material world into greater consonance with the spiritual by the medium of earnest work (like the bridge his father had built), or, to vary the metaphor, to make the material world more transparent so that the spiritual can be discerned through it. This is a mission imposed upon man by his nature. Any attempt to elude it (for example, by pursuing nothing but the satisfaction of one's own appetites and vanities, or by caring purely for the appearance of one's work rather for its solid worth) is blasphemous and, ultimately, self-destructive. Man, therefore, works in the material world, but it is crucial that his efforts should be guided and illuminated by a sense of the spiritual reality underlying it, a sense that is all too easily and frequently lacking. In a healthy society, all men will feel it naturally; but already in *Sartor* there is visible the germ of an alternative idea that was grow out of all proportion in Carlyle's later work, the idea of 'hero-worship'.

This was something that Carlyle had learned in the first place from Fichte, with his idea of the 'learned man' as the interpreter of the Ideal to the mass of men unable to discern it for

themselves. For Carlyle similarly the Hero performs the traditional role of the Priest, the interpreter of God's will to man.
The Priest himself was no longer available for this role, for Carlyle never recovered his faith in orthodox Christianity, and to
him all existing Churches and religions were systems of cant, of
organised hypocrisy, professing beliefs which they no longer
sincerely held, worshipping symbols which had in their time
been valid but which had now become hollow shells. But the
Hero in any case was a broader concept than the Priest. In
*Sartor Resartus* he is still primarily the writer and teacher, as he
had been in Fichte; but he can also be the king, and later Carlyle was to recognise him in still other roles. But his essence is
still to be the messenger of the divine to men. He has insight into
the ultimate spiritual reality to which most men are blind, and
all good men – in a good society, all men – will sense the fact,
following him willingly, because only in conformity to the dic-
tates of that ultimate spiritual reality does freedom lie.

These are the common themes of all Carlyle's writings after
*Sartor*; and, looked at in the cold light of day, they may well
seem a nebulous and unremarkable lot, affording a poor foun-
dation for any claim to greatness for their author. They are not
more than lukewarm German Idealism, crossed with a dash of
Carlyle's native Puritanism. The criticism can only be accepted;
indeed, it must be taken further. Carlyle's whole bent of mind
was antipathetic to precision of argument and to systematic
reasoning. That he was *capable* of these things has to be
accepted – he had, after all, been a geometer of distinction in
his Edinburgh days; but one seeks in vain in his writings for
any passage of close reasoning. It is impossible to make any
serious claim for him as a philosopher (nor, indeed, did he
make it for himself). Already in *Sartor* his tendency to prefer
vague metaphysical uplift to analytical rigour is disconcertingly
apparent, as may be detected easily enough in the foregoing
summary of his ideas. Moreover, as we have seen, he was not
even an accurate transmitter of the ideas of his German mentors. He repeatedly distorted and coarsened their distinctions
and definitions, usually in the interest of deriving a simpler
moral message from them; and it is most unlikely that Kant,
Fichte, or perhaps even Goethe, would have recognised the

'Philosophy of Clothes' of *Sartor* as a legitimate deduction from their ideas. Carlyle's habitual method was to seize on isolated ideas and phrases from their work – *Entsagen* (renunciation), *Selbsttodtung* (self-annihilation), *Ernst ist das Leben* ('Life is earnest'), and so on – lift them out of context, and reinterpret them in ways that suited him, which is certainly not a widely approved recipe for constructive academic enquiry.

But *Sartor* cannot be assessed purely in terms of its academic content, and this has been recognised during the century and a half since it was written by the way in which it has been quietly handed over from the realm of philosophy to that of literature. Carlyle habitually thought with his imagination, jumping from one association to another. His genius lies, not in conducting his readers along a carefully-graduated series of argumentative steps towards an irresistible conclusion, but in putting two or more seemingly very different objects or situations unexpectedly next to each other, in sudden and blinding juxtaposition, and forcing the reader, even unwillingly, to recognise likenesses where he had seen none before. It was in the realm of the imagination that his supreme talent lay, and *Sartor Resartus* marks a critical point of his development because it was here that he first fully recognised and published the fact. In his essay of 1827 on the 'State of German Literature' he had been at pains to establish the central, Kantian distinction of German Idealism, between *Vernunft* and *Verstand* – Understanding and Reason, as Coleridge had Englished them. In *Sartor* this distinction nowhere appears (nor does it reappear in later works). It is replaced by a broader distinction between logic on the one hand, and intuition and imagination on the other, to the invariable advantage of the latter. 'Wouldst thou plant for Eternity,' he says, 'then plant into the deep infinite faculties of man, his Fantasy and Heart; wouldst thou plant for Year and Day, then plant into his shallow superficial faculties, his Self-love and Arithmetical Understanding, what will grow there' (S 179).

These claims for the primacy of the imagination are not wholly original. They had been anticipated, in particular, by the first two generations of English Romantic poets, by Wordsworth, Coleridge, Keats and Shelley. But there is no evidence that Carlyle's ideas were derived from them, and although during his

residence in London in 1824–5 he was for a time on the fringe
of the circle that imbibed Coleridge's Idealism from the lips of
the ageing poet at Highgate, he showed little interest in their
work. From his own experience, Carlyle derived a conviction of
the fundamental importance of the hidden depths in human nature, accessible not to the persuasions of reason and calculation,
but only by appeals to the imagination, above all through the
use of symbols. In his brilliant essay from the same period,
'Characteristics', the central theme is the superiority of the unconscious element in man to the conscious, a theme crystallised
in a series of memorable epigrams: 'In our inward, as in our
outward world, what is mechanical lies open to us; not what is
dynamical and has vitality'; 'Manufacture is intelligible, but tri-
vial: Creation is great, and cannot be understood' (E III 4,5). At
times, in his best work of the 1830s, Carlyle can be felt groping
intuitively for concepts of the subconscious mind and the mass
unconscious that have had to wait for the twentieth century for
their development. These doctrines, of the primacy of the unconscious and of thinking with the imagination, have come into
bad odour in this century, because of their associations with
totalitarianism, especially in its Nazi and Fascist forms. In the
1940s Carlyle was not uncommonly put into the dock as one of
the intellectual ancestors of Fascism, and for the later Carlyle
there may be some truth in the charge; of the Carlyle of *Sartor*
and the 1830s, it is true only in so far as he adumbrated some
truths about human nature of which Fascism was later to make
brilliant and wicked use.

There is another sense also in which *Sartor* heralds a defini-
tive change in the direction of Carlyle's thinking. Mention has
already been made of a growing interest in social issues which
can be discerned in his choice of topics for his periodical articles. In 'Signs of the Times' in 1829, and then in 'Characteristics' in 1831, he had appeared in the new role of social critic.
This is not something he had learned from the Germans, and
indeed there is little sign of it in him before 1829. It is true that
the subjects of his review articles, imposed upon him by the
editors of the periodicals, afforded small opportunity for social
criticism; but it is absent even from his correspondence. As
the educated son of a poor man, and as one who both felt

and resented the difficulty of wringing acceptance for himself and his views out of the literary establishment, he might seem to have the equipment of an angry young man; the example of Cobbett shows the opportunities that existed for social criticism in the years of bitter hardship and social tension between 1815 and 1821. But Carlyle at this time was wrapped in his personal agonies, and apart from one fleeting glimpse in the *Reminiscences* he wrote in his old age, there is nothing to show that he took any part in the conflicts of that time. Carlyle's advocacy of German literature did however lead him to a low estimate of the English society which so grossly underestimated it and at the same time so signally failed (in his eyes) to produce any worthwhile literature of its own. 'Signs of the Times', his first general indictment of contemporary society, already reveals his remarkable ability to identify the characteristics of a society's moral and intellectual condition – an art all the more difficult when, as here, it is a contemporary society that is being described. In 'Signs of the Times' it is the prevailing emphasis upon mechanism, both literal and metaphorical, that he seizes upon as typical of the age: 'Men are grown mechanical in head and in heart, as well as in hand. They have lost faith in individual endeavour, and in natural force, of any kind. Not for internal perfection, but for external combinations and arrangements, for institutions, constitutions – for Mechanism of one sort or another, do they hope and struggle' (E II 63). This emphasis upon the mechanical to the exclusion of the dynamic, the neglect of the unconscious and instinctive sources from which human creativity springs, was for Carlyle a sure sign of disease. There is also an implication here of an organic notion of society which, although never consistently held, is nevertheless typical of much of Carlyle's social criticism. Society is not a mere collection of individuals, but a living entity which can be healthy or sick as a whole. This mode of thinking, which he had undoubtedly learned from his German reading, is fundamentally opposed to the individualism of the Enlightenment. At this time, though, the criticism of society is confined to its intellectual tendencies; there is nothing as yet about economic hardship or social conditions.

The same is true of the more far-reaching and ambitious

essay on 'Characteristics', written in the autumn of 1831; but by this time Carlyle's attitude to social problems was undergoing a change, due chiefly, it seems, to two influences. In the summer of 1830 he had come into contact with the Saint-Simonians, a group of idealistic young reformers in Paris who curiously combined a demand for a new religion with a demand for far-reaching social reform. The combination, though, was attractive to Carlyle. In the winter of 1830–1 he went so far as to translate *Le Nouveau Christianisme*, the key work of Saint-Simon, the group's founder. His translation was never published, and his contact with the group was short-lived. Goethe advised him against it, and Carlyle himself had never been able to swallow their strange synthetic brand of religion; but it does appear that they played some part in directing his attention to poverty as one of the most prominent and menacing problems of contemporary society.

The second influence working in this direction is less questionable: it was the experience of living in London in the winter of 1831–2, a period of severe social distress when the Reform Bill crisis was at its height. His letters are full of the issue, and there is no doubt now where his sympathies lie. Carlyle was always at his best in the presence of suffering; there could be a surface grimness in his manner, but beneath it there was a very tender heart (during the 1830s he was never anything but a poor man, but his correspondence often contains references to small private acts of charity, usually anonymous).

The hardships of the poor, as he became aware of them in London that winter, touched him; but they did more than that. He began to see the gratuitous suffering inflicted upon the poor, through no fault of their own, as an injustice for which society, and in particular the ruling classes, would have to answer bitterly. An apocalyptic note begins for the first time to creep into his writings. Already in 'Signs of the Times' he had recognised that 'there is a deep-lying struggle in the whole fabric of society; a boundless grinding collision of the New with the Old' (E II 182). Already in 'Characteristics' he had declared that 'the Physical derangements of Society are but the image and impress of its Spiritual' (E III 22). Now, in *Sartor*, he is never more at one with Teufelsdrockh than in the scene in the

Green Goose tavern in Weissnichtwo where the philosopher raises his beer-mug and, to thunderous applause, proclaims 'The Cause of the Poor, in God's name and the Devil's!' (S 11).

In the later chapters of the book he proclaims his admiration for only two human types, the inspired artist and the 'toilworn Craftsman'. He declares the decadence of a society in which the poor perish 'like neglected, foundered Draught-Cattle, of Hunger and Overwork' (S 185); and, with a savagery learnt from Swift, he proposes as a cure for over-population an annual three days' hunting season for the shooting of paupers. 'The expense were trifling: nay the very carcasses would pay it. Have them salted and barrelled; could you not victual therewith, if not Army and Navy, yet richly such infirm Paupers, in workhouses and elsewhere, as enlightened Charity, dreading no evil of them, might see good to keep alive?' (S 183). In his 'Dandies' and 'Drudges' he anticipates the class divisions which were to form one of the major themes of *Past and Present*. There was a formidable indignation at social injustice rising in *Sartor Resartus*; and in the years that followed it was to become the keynote of the message that Carlyle felt himself called to announce to England.

# 3 Recognition

The publication of *Sartor Resartus* marked an epoch in Carlyle's own intellectual development. It did not mark the achievement of any widespread public recognition. For the next three years the Carlyles, settled now in their house in Cheyne Row, lived very thriftily; the household was kept afloat by Jane's sharp-eyed housekeeping, while her husband set himself to the history of the French Revolution which for some years now had been looming up in his mind. Carlyle several times looked, always in vain, for some regular employment which might provide a little more financial security while he worked on the book; these were years, too, of recurring afflictions, neurotic or otherwise – biliousness for him, headaches for her, sleeplessness for both. Writing was always as much an agony as a necessity for Carlyle. His correspondence rings with his groans over the difficulty of obtaining books, the dullness and obtuseness of his sources, the sense of an immense burden laid upon him, the mental darkness through which he had to grope his way in trying to shape his material. Yet in many ways they were happy years. The Carlyles picked up again the threads of the friendships they had formed in London in 1831–2, and to both of them the opportunity for companionship with men and women of their own tastes, interests and abilities came like a breath of life after the rustic isolation of Craigenputtock. Carlyle had a genius for friendship; this is perhaps less true of Jane, but she had an immense zest for companionship, and in her own right ranked high among the most brilliant and witty talkers in London. In combination they were irresistible, her wit setting off Carlyle's intense moral earnestness and broad humour; and there rapidly gathered around them a coterie of the best minds and literary talents in London, especially those of the rising generation.

The twin decisions to settle in London and to start work on *The French Revolution* can be seen now to have represented the final point of decision for Carlyle; coming as they did almost at the mid-point of his life, they determined the direction that the rest of it would take. In the words that Carlyle used to describe a similar crisis in the life of his friend John Sterling, 'a crisis in life had come; when, of innumerable possibilities, one possibility was to be elected king, and swallow all the rest' (J 71). For Carlyle the alternative possibilities were, if not innumerable, at least very numerous: he might have been mathematician, moral philosopher, literary critic, perhaps civil servant. But the decision to write *The French Revolution* confirmed that it was as a historian, a moralist and a social critic that Carlyle was to establish his public reputation; and he and Jane were to live and die in Cheyne Row.

Carlyle's increasing absorption, in the years before 1834, in the problems of British society makes the continued importance of this theme in his work unsurprising. But his appearance as a historian calls for more comment, for of his writings before 1834 only the essay on 'Count Cagliostro', which appeared in 1833, and the two essays on history of 1830 and 1833 could be described as falling within this field. Many of his review essays, certainly, had shown a considerable knowledge of the eighteenth-century background, and an interest in relating the authors he was discussing to the moral and intellectual condition of the society in which they worked; but fundamentally they remained within the field of literary criticism. Nevertheless, Carlyle's interest in history was life-long, and he had read deeply in it since his university days. If he had not published any historical works hitherto, this was mainly because the urgent demands, first of finding a way out of his own spiritual crisis, and then of accommodating himself to the demands of review editors in order to make a living, had diverted him in a different direction. Even so, in 1821 he did considerable reading with a view to writing a history of the English seventeenth-century Civil War and Commonwealth – a theme which was to haunt him until it finally found expression in his *Oliver Cromwell* a quarter of a century later; we have just seen that in 1830 he was contemplating a book on Luther; and in the winter of 1833–4 the rival possibilities of books on either Knox or the French Revolution were jostling each other for priority in his mind. It is clear, therefore, that the decision to devote himself entirely to the writing of a major historical work did not in itself involve any great change

of direction for Carlyle. Nevertheless, we must look very closely
at his notion of what history was and how it should be written,
for it was a very idiosyncratic notion indeed and was to give rise
to a very idiosyncratic book.

Carlyle saw history on an enormously broad canvas: he was
capable of claiming, not only that history was 'the most profit-
able of all studies', but even that 'History is not only the fittest
study, but the only study, and includes all others whatsoever'
(E III 167, 168). Within these claims, it seems possible to identify two main, and contrasting, reasons why history came to
take on this transcendent importance for him. In the first place,
he had a quite exceptionally acute private awareness of the mys-
teriousness of Time as the transparent medium in which all human action is irretrievably stuck. He was haunted by the contrast between the lightning-fast transiency of experience and the
utter impossibility of re-entering the past to retrieve it; this
vision very strongly conditioned his historical writing. Some of
this Time-mysticism he learned from Goethe – he frequently
illustrated it by reference to the song of the Earth-Spirit from
*Faust* – but it seems impossible to believe that it was not also
natural to him, so often does he revert to the theme and so vivid
is his expression of it. His regular visits in later life to the
scenes of his childhood in Annandale became to him experi-
ences of almost unbearable pathos because of this awareness,
and are most movingly described in his letters. One of his main
preoccupations in writing history was precisely the attempt to
recover the lost past and to make it live again.

But history had another, and perhaps even greater, significance for Carlyle: it was a gospel, the revelation of a just providence working in human affairs. Not, certainly, a gospel that
could be read simplistically; in the essay 'On History' he bids
the historian 'pause over the mysterious vestiges of Him, whose
path is in the great deep of Time, *whom History indeed reveals,
but only all History, and in Eternity, will clearly reveal*' (E II 89,
my italics); but it is nevertheless perhaps the most clearly-legible
gospel for nineteenth-century man. Carlyle never recovered the
simple faith in the Bible that his parents' generation had possessed, deeply though he revered it; nor did his recovery of faith
through the medium of German Idealism in the 1820s give him

any comparable source of revelation. Rather, his faith that the workings of a just providence could be traced in history gave him a creed of his own – though certainly one that had more in common with the Puritanism of his ancestors than with the ideas of any of his German mentors.

It was, all the same, a creed that could be given an acceptably 'Germanic' colouring, by seeing in this revelation of providence in history another case of the Ideal manifesting itself in the Real. In thus replacing a faith in the Bible with a faith in History, Carlyle had good nineteenth-century company – most notably, Hegel and Marx, though he was never aware of the parallel. Nor, indeed, is the parallel by any means complete, since to both Hegel and Marx history was a progressive phenomenon. The theme of progress does sometimes occur in Carlyle's writings (especially the earlier ones), but it is very muted and eventually disappears altogether. To Hegel partially and to Marx wholly, history was an autonomous and self-justifying process; to Carlyle it was something more like a theatre for the workings of a providence which itself remains firmly outside history, and whose main concern is less to steer history as a whole to some satisfactory conclusion than to punish and counter the misdeeds and follies of human beings and human societies. Here too, though, Carlyle is inconsistent, and fluctuates between a providential view of history and a more naturalistic one, gleaned from Goethe and the Saint-Simonians, according to which societies oscillate between ages of faith and ages of unbelief. But on the whole Carlyle was much less concerned with laws of history that could not be broken than with rules of history that must not be. He was a less radical historical thinker than Hegel or Marx, and his view has as much in common with the Book of Kings as it does with a fully naturalistic scheme of history like Marx's. But he does share, if in a somewhat confused way, the typical nineteenth-century perception of time as the most significant dimension of both the natural and the human world – a perception exemplified not only by thinkers like Hegel and Marx, but, perhaps even more significantly, by scientists like the evolutionary geologists of the first half of the century and the evolutionary biologists of the second.

It is the providential view, though, that increasingly comes out on top from the mid-1830s onward; this, of course imparts a great importance to the study of history, for, from the example of the chastisements that have been visited upon erring societies in the past, existing societies can learn to mend their ways in the present. It was on these grounds that Carlyle proclaimed the identity of history and prophecy: the Church had lost its function as the authentic interpreter of God to men and had become a mere hypocritical sham in which sincere belief was impossible. History was now the true revelation of the divine, and the inspired historian was the prophet. Carlyle went further than this: he claimed that history was not only the prophecy, but the poetry, of the modern age. Poetry for Carlyle had little to do with the writing of verse, an activity of which he had a low estimate (he thought that both Tennyson and Browning, in common with all other contemporary poets, would have done better to write prose). Its function was to take a portion of the Real, and by force of imagination to make the Ideal show through it. This, he held, was the true nature of all creative work; and in so far as history was the supreme epitome of human experience, the writing of history represented the highest form of poetry. This eccentric claim makes more sense if seen in the context of the peculiar qualities of Carlyle's genius. His supreme faculty was the imagination, and it dominated his thinking. Since the imagination is the great Romantic faculty, this justifies us in seeing Carlyle as one of the central figures of English Romanticism; central, but not typical, because the literary forms in which the Romantic imagination found most natural expression were poetry and the novel. Carlyle attempted both in his youth, but found both alien to him. His love of the concrete and the actual, as opposed to the fictional, led him to history; and he found the solution to his problem of self-expression in writing a kind of history based not, as it usually has been, on the reasoning faculty, but on the imagination. In terms of his own experience, at any rate, the claim to have united poetry and history makes sense and can be justified.

Carlyle seems to have held two different underlying theories of the nature of historical writing, which may not be incompatible but certainly have no necessary connection. On the one hand, his own sensibility, reinforced by his German reading,

led him to a mystical view of time and to the idea that the
function of the historian is the literal recreation of the vanished
past in the imagination of the reader. He once wrote, 'the great
business for me, in which alone I feel any comfort, is recording
the *presence*, bodily concrete coloured presence of things' (T IX
15). On the other hand, history was the revelation of providence, and the business of the historian was to interpret this
revelation and to bring his readers to apply it to their own time
and circumstances. Carlyle himself was not aware of the incon-
sistency; and, remarkably, in *The French Revolution* he achieved
a real fusion of the two. This feat required a very high imaginative temperature, which he never fully achieved in his later historical writings, where the prophetic, admonitory element becomes more and more dominant. Both conceptions of history
are far apart from those commonly current either at the time or
now. Carlyle did not believe that the historian's function was to
provide a smoothly flowing narrative for the entertainment of
his readers, nor that history could be treated as an experimental
science from which inductive laws of human behaviour could be
derived, nor that rigid objectivity and detachment were either
possible or desirable qualities in a historian. He defied every
established canon of his own day as to how history should be
written, and every canon that has been established since; and he
wrote a masterpiece.

The choice of the French Revolution as his subject was in no
way accidental, though, as we have seen, he had earlier considered writing on other historical subjects. But increasingly in
the years before 1834 the French Revolution was shaping itself
in his mind as the central fact of modern history. There was of
course nothing very unusual in this perception. Fear of the Revolution and of the ideas that it had propagated was widespread
among the upper classes of the Continent after 1815, and to a
lesser extent this was true of Britain also. But to Carlyle, the
Revolution was primarily a cause of hope rather than fear; for it
was a sentence of divine justice on a corrupt society. This was
an interpretation rooted deep in Carlyle's own values and in his
spiritual history. The eighteenth century, to him, was the age of
unbelief, of scepticism, of destructive criticism, the monstrous
negatives which had inflicted upon him that dark night of the

soul during his youth at Edinburgh. The brilliant intellectual culture of the French Enlightenment was the source from which it all came, or, to use a more appropriate metaphor, the patch of desert which gradually extended itself over the whole Continent; in the Revolution it got what it deserved. 'I would not have known what to make of the world, if it had not been for the French Revolution,' he once said (FF II 18). There is no doubt an element of *Schadenfreude* in this. Carlyle never liked France; the hostility can be seen even in his accounts of his first brief visit to Paris with the Bullers in 1824, and, together with his counterposed admiration for Germany, can be traced right through his life, up to his exultation at the German victory over France in 1871. The dislike was due more than anything to the fact that, in a way very typical of Carlyle, he saw France as a symbol, a symbol of an intellectual and moral tradition that he abhorred.

*The French Revolution* took three years to write. To Carlyle writing was always an agonising business. *The French Revolution* in fact flowed more easily from him than either of his two later major historical works, *Oliver Cromwell* and *Frederick the Great*, and its superior spontaneity is very apparent; but it still cost an immense effort. Much of this can be traced to its dependence on his imagination, a capricious faculty far less under the control of the will than is the reason, and some of it to the difficulty of coupling the imagination to the materials of history. Carlyle was an extremely diligent and conscientious researcher, who habitually went to immense lengths to check the accuracy of his information. But, rather than coming to his research with a set of questions thought out in advance and arranging and categorising his materials systematically as he read, his method was to digest all the material available, shut it up in his imagination and let it ferment there; then, when the process was complete, it would boil out spontaneously in the form his imagination had given to it. He himself compared the process to the eruption of a volcano; and waiting for the moment of eruption could be long and agonising, all the more so because the book commonly seemed to him worthless while he was writing it. In addition, there were external problems that even a conventional historian might have found daunting. There was a constant struggle to make ends meet. His researches were greatly limited by the fact that he could not afford a trip to Paris, and hence had to work entirely from printed sources available in England; and on top of that, he was unable to make use of the British Museum's unrivalled collection of French Revolutionary pamphlets, owing to a quarrel with the vain and irritable librarian, Panizzi. To crown everything, when the first (of three) volumes was complete in manuscript, and was lent to John Stuart Mill (who more than anyone had encouraged him to undertake the work) to read, by some accident it was mistaken for waste paper and burnt. Carlyle had destroyed all his notes; but real calamity called out the best in him, as it always did. His immediate reaction was sympathy for the shattered and inconsolable Mill, who insisted on paying Carlyle for the time lost in working on the volume. Then, with a resolution that deserves to be called heroic, he sat down and rewrote it.

*The French Revolution* was published in 1837. It was preceded by two lengthy narrative essays, 'The Diamond Necklace' and 'Mirabeau', themselves sufficiently remarkable, which can be seen as by-products of his work on the book. 'The Diamond Necklace', in particular, anticipates many of the characteristic narrative devices of *The French Revolution*. But inevitably it was the book itself which attracted most attention. It was not an instantaneous popular success, which is not surprising, for Carlyle had made no concessions to his readers; but the reviews were generally favourable, and some very distinguished literary figures, Thackeray outstanding among them, were outspoken from the first in their verdict that, beneath all its shocking originalities of form and style, the book was a masterpiece. The sales gradually gathered way, and Carlyle's reputation with them. *The French Revolution* certainly did not make Carlyle a rich man (he never was one); but it gave him an established literary reputation and status that he never lost, and to its abler readers it spoke a message that they had, consciously or unconsciously, been long waiting for, and that many of them remembered to the end of their lives.

*The French Revolution* is a very strange history indeed. It is, to begin with, a work of high Romantic art, which means that, far more than any normal work of history, it cannot be detached

from its author. 'The Book is one of the *savagest* written for
several centuries', Carlyle himself said; 'it is a book written by a
*wild man*, a man disunited from the fellowship of the world he
lives in: looking King and beggar in the face with an indifference of brotherhood, an indifference of contempt' (FL I 96).
Contempt always came somewhat too easily to Carlyle, and
there is an element of posing here; nevertheless it is not an un-
fair comment on the book, and its implication that the book is
primarily a projection of the author is revealing. Carlyle does
not attempt orthodox narrative, which he always distrusted.
One of the most penetrating epigrams ever uttered about history is his 'Narrative is *linear*, Action is *solid!*' (E II 89); and his
solution to this problem is to break up his account of the Revolution into a series of marvellously vivid scenes of present
action separated by great gulfs of darkness, periods which he
passes over rapidly with the merest summary of events. This
effect of extreme discontinuity reflects his own conviction that
large areas of history are best forgotten. The historian's job is to
concentrate on those which can still be brought alive for the
present. The impression on the reader is one of violent chiaros-
curo, ideally suited to reflect the lurid events of the Revolution.
Carlyle's old patron Francis Jeffrey very accurately described it
as 'like reading history by flashes of lightning'. Few history
books, if any, have ever so perfectly matched style and subject,
for Carlyle's style is itself a revolution, a deliberate wrenching
break with the entire Augustan tradition of English prose writing, and in its exaggerations, its grotesqueries and its violent
discontinuities exactly mirrors the events it describes. The style
was subjected to strong criticism at the time, by Sterling among
others, but Carlyle's reply to him was forceful: 'Do you reckon
this really a time for purism of style? I do not. With the struc-
ture of our Johnsonian English breaking up from its foundations, revolution *there* is visible as everywhere else' (T VIII 135).
Moreover, the effect of the style is reinforced by equally violent
contrasts of scale, of close-up and distant landscape. In the
midst of a lurid description of the horrors following the storming of the Bastille (one of the most famous descriptions of violence ever written), Carlyle is capable of varying his focus like
this:

One other officer is massacred; one other Invalide is hanged on, the Lamp-iron; with difficulty, with generous persever-ance, the Gardes Francaises will save the rest. Provost Fles-selles, stricken long since with the paleness of death, must descend from his seat, 'to be judged at the Palais Royal': – alas, to be shot dead, by an unknown hand, at the turning of the first street!

O evening sun of July, how, at this hour, thy beams fall slant on reapers amid peaceful woody fields; on old women spin-ning in cottages; on ships far out in the silent main; on Balls at the Orangerie of Versailles, where high-rouged Dames of the Palace are even now dancing with double-jacketed Hussar-Officers . . . (R I 197)

It is a cinematic effect; abruptly, the camera soars away into the blue, till all France is spread out below it, and the chaos around the Bastille is only one speck of violent action in a land-scape deep in the peace of a summer evening. Carlyle never allows the reader's attention to become totally concentrated on one plane. He is forever reminding you that, against the furious scenes of public action that capture the attention of the histor-ian, there have to be set, on the one hand the multitude of private lives going quietly on, unaffected by the storm, on the other the enormous perspectives of past and future time.

The vividness of the descriptions is extraordinary. This was a characteristic of Carlyle's conversation. He always had the cari-caturist's gift of dashing off a face, a character, a scene in a single compressed, pithy phrase, and he never made better use of it than in *The French Revolution*. His use of the present tense throughout thrusts both writer and reader into the thick of the action, questioning the actors, admonishing them, reconstruct-ing the moment-by-moment revelations of a new turn of events. To an astonishing extent he actually achieves his aim, not merely to present his readers with 'hearsays of things', that is, conventional narrative, nor to pass easy judgement on them, but to thrust those readers into the 'bodily concrete coloured presence' of events, and to force them to make up their minds for themselves. Russell Lowell commented appositely that Car-lyle's figures are so real that 'if you prick them, they bleed'.

A full analysis of the dazzling array of literary techniques that Carlyle deploys in *The French Revolution* would be a major undertaking; but there is one other device so characteristic of his habits of thought that we cannot overlook it. Carlyle lays great stress on the social importance of symbols. As we have seen, he drew from his acquaintance with German thought the idea that the Ideal can only be mediated to man through the Real – that is, through symbols. Thus, Church and King are both supremely important symbols; and nothing shows better the corruption of French society in the eighteenth century than the fact that both have become hollow, have lost their symbolical force. But symbolism penetrates Carlyle's historical method itself. Book II, 'The Paper Age', is constructed round the symbol of paper: paper money, with no sufficient bullion backing; paper schemes of reform, with no prospects of being put into effect; and, as the climax, ascending from Reveillon's paper-warehouse, the brothers Montgolfiers' paper balloon, the perfect symbol of French society in the 1780s – full of hot air, unable to steer, and liable to explode. It is a dazzling piece of historiographical virtuosity; the symbol works perfectly, and involves no straining of the facts. As a historical method, it may be called arbitrary and subjective; but it shows, as few other historians have ever done, the possibilities of a historiography prepared to make full use of all the resources of a first-rate imagination.

To write a great Romantic masterpiece of the creative imagination without ever straying outside the limits of scrupulously accurate history is a very remarkable achievement indeed. But it was the intellectual content of *The French Revolution* that contemporaries found most important, and the ideas it expressed had much to do with Carlyle's establishment as a social prophet.

Carlyle presented what, to English readers at any rate, was a wholly novel interpretation of the Revolution. In the 1830s, the Revolution was still a thing of horror and unredeemed evil to educated opinion in this country; a mere volcanic upsurge of brutal violence, terrifying as a precedent, and associated with a political creed of radical democracy abhorred by all right-thinking men. Carlyle did not deny the horror and the violence – he takes no sides – and he was never at any stage of his life a

democrat. But to him, all the horrors of the Revolution were no
more than the natural outcome of all that had gone before.
They were judgement visited on a society which had lost touch
with the divine realities; a society which had denied its gods, in
which all the old symbols of the transcendent had become trans-
parently hollow shams, in which above all the ruling class had
forgotten its divinely-ordained responsibilities to those over
whom it was commissioned to rule, remembering only its privileges and its pleasures. This is a theme which stands out
strongly and unambiguously in the first volume of *The French
Revolution*. The menacing growl of the unfed poor is present as
a ground-swell in the background of all the earlier chapters.
The point of departure for the book is Louis XV's deathbed –
fittingly, since death to Carlyle is the supremest and stern-
est of all destroyers of illusions – and the king's flattering
nickname, 'Louis the Well-Beloved', is ironically counterposed
against the state of his kingdom, with its 'lank scarecrows, that
prowl hunger-stricken through all highways and byways of
French Existence' and 'in the Bicetre Hospital, "eight to a
bed", lie waiting their manumission' (R I 5). The theme recurs
in Carlyle's narration of Louis XV's encounter, while out hunting, with a peasant with a coffin: '"For whom?" – It was for a
poor brother slave, whom Majesty had sometimes noticed slav-
ing in those quarters. "What did he die of?" – "Of hunger": –
the King gave his steed the spur' (R I 19). Hunger, bankruptcy
and death are the realities that stare more and more visibly
through the ragged splendours of the Old Regime in the first
three books of the first volume, realities which the regime tries
in vain to ignore; they are the machinery through which the
divine justice works itself out. The end of them, inevitably, is
violent revolution; and when the first appalling lynchings take
place in the streets of Paris – the sort of horrors that dominated
the English image of the Revolution – Carlyle's comment is
'Horrible, in Lands that had known equal justice! Not so un-
natural in Lands that had never known it' (R I 208).

This was strong meat for English readers of the 1830s – too
strong for a good many of them, to whom it seemed that Carlyle
was abetting violence, at a time when violence was all too con-
ceivable, even within England itself. Indeed, Carlyle's inter-

pretation of the years leading up to 1789 as a time of steadily increasing hardship for the poor has not stood up well to later historical research; but this is hardly the main point. *The French Revolution* was original in that it was the first major attempt in English both to put the Revolution into an intelligible historical context, rather than representing it as a monstrosity at odds with nature; and, on the moral level, to suggest that the old monarchical and aristocratic regime in France deserved what it got, that the economic and political crises that finally led up to the Revolution were only the symptoms of a fundamental moral failure on the part of the French ruling class. But the suggestion that a ruling class lives, so to speak, under judgement, and a judgement that sooner or later will work itself out, not in the comfortable distance of an afterlife, but here and now on earth, was a radical and dangerous one in the 1830s. It was one to attract daring and radical minds as much as it frightened middle-aged and conservative ones; and all the more when the parallel between eighteenth-century France and nineteenth-century Britain was so clearly intended by the author.

The sympathy with the suffering and neglected poor that runs through the early books of *The French Revolution* is, unmistakably, the result of Carlyle's observations in London during the winter of 1831–2. Throughout the 1830s the consciousness of social distress is one of the most consistent themes of his correspondence – a distress interpreted in the same terms of neglect by the ruling class as he employed in his analysis of events in France, and which he saw as bound to lead in the end to some similar catastrophe. The lesson was driven home to him by the difficulties of his own family, struggling to make a living on the land in Dumfriesshire. One of his brothers, Alexander, was finally forced to emigrate to Canada, and in the late 1830s Carlyle himself also thought very seriously more than once of emigrating to America. The comparison with contemporary England is always present in the background of *The French Revolution*. It is usually tacit, but no acute reader was likely to miss the ominous parallels between the condition of the French working-classes in the eighteenth century as described by Carlyle, and the condition of the English working-classes of the 1830s – the desperate agricultural distress and widespread rioting of 1830–1, the Reform Bill riots of the following year, the persecution of the Tolpuddle Martyrs, the renewed distress caused by the onset of economic depression after 1837 and reflected in the rise of the Chartist movement; nor between a parasitic French aristocracy clinging to its position of privilege, and an English aristocracy hated for its resistance to the Reform Bill and for its adamant refusal to modify the commercial and hunting privileges conferred upon it by the Corn Laws and the Game Laws. There were a good many intelligent observers in the England of the late 1830s who thought that revolution was a real possibility. *The French Revolution* reflected both that fear and the rising moral disquiet that many of them felt as to the justice of the existing social order. Nor was Carlyle's comparison between old France and present England always tacit. There is a remarkable passage in which he discusses the fate of the boy Dauphin, Louis XVI's heir, who died in prison in obscure circumstances after his father's execution. This was a topic that lent itself easily to sentiment, and over which many easy English tears had been shed. Carlyle himself does not conceal his sympathy for the boy, but he has something to say to the shedders of the tears too:

> The poor boy, hidden in a tower of the Temple, from which in his fright and bewilderment and early decrepitude he wishes not to stir out, lies perishing, 'his shirt not changed for six months'; amid squalor and darkness, lamentably, – so as none but poor Factory Children and the like are wont to perish, and *not* be lamented! (R III 263).

The soft-hearted reader has his hypocrisy suddenly thrust brutally under his eyes. Even a century and a half later, it is hard to avoid recoiling at the savagery with which Carlyle turns on him.

To Carlyle, the Revolution was the great standing demonstration that, whatever appearances there might be to the contrary, the world was indeed ruled in the last resort by a just providence. The book was intended, and widely read, as a proclamation of this truth to his own countrymen, that they might learn it and apply it to their own country while there was yet time. In this sense *The French Revolution* is a sermon; but it is a rich and complex book, and cannot be reduced to a single formula.

Carlyle himself said that he put more of his life into it than into any of his other books, and it has indeed all the compression to be expected of an imaginative mind of the highest class at last finding full, free and coherent expression after half a lifetime of confinement and frustration. Carlyle was forty-one before *The French Revolution* finally established his reputation; and there is a curious parallel between his own position at the time and the portrait he draws of the popular leader Mirabeau at the opening of the States-General in 1789. Of all the immense gallery of vividly-drawn characters in *The French Revolution*, Mirabeau is the only one to whom Carlyle accords full heroic status. The choice is curious, for Mirabeau's influence on events was never decisive, and his early death soon removed him from the scene; it is tempting to see the explanation in an awareness on Carlyle's part, whether conscious or subconscious, of the parallel between Mirabeau's career and his own up to that time:

> In fiery rough figure, with black Samson-locks under the slouch-hat, he steps along there. A fiery fuliginous mass, which could not be choked and smothered, but would fill all France with smoke. And now it has got *air*; it will burn its whole substance, its whole smoke-atmosphere too, and fill all France with flame. Strange lot! Forty years of that smoulder-ing, with foul fire-damp and vapour enough; then victory over that; – and like a burning mountain he blazes heaven-high; and, for twenty-three resplendent months, pours out, in flame and molten fire-torrents, all that is in him, the Pha-ros and Wonder-sign of an amazed Europe; – and then lies hollow, cold for ever! (R I 140–1)

*Sartor Resartus* had been an almost wholly, even self-indulgently, personal document. After 1837, all Carlyle's writ-ings for thirty years were to be almost wholly public ones. *The French Revolution* uniquely combined the two; and this, if it sometimes confuses the themes of the book, gives it an extraor-dinary resonance, because the public reference so often echoes, and is given urgency by, a private reference within it which the reader can sense; the book is at one and the same time a work of objective history and of Romantic self-expression, as perhaps no other history book has ever been. The passage on Mirabeau just cited is an obvious example of this: another instance, on a much greater scale, may be the treatment of the Terror, the period of arbitrary arrests and mass executions that marked the climax of the Revolution in 1793–4. The third and last volume of *The French Revolution* is shaped entirely round the unifying concept of the Terror, which in Carlyle's hands becomes a living entity with a brutal but wholly irresistible life of its own, quite independent of the lives of the individuals, the Dantons and Robespierres, whom it first uses and then destroys with equal indifference. It is a vast, horrifying, phantasmagoric, irresistible, awe-inspiring, totally authentic thing; something which defies all moral categories: 'worthy of horror, worthy of worship'. On the rational level, this at least represents a more realistic analysis than the level of easy dismissal and condemnation which had been the current British attitude to the Terror before Carlyle wrote; and it clearly fits adequately into the overriding interpretation of the Revolution as a judgement on a corrupt society. Yet one can feel a deeper level of meaning than this in the intensity of Carlyle's picture of the Terror; it is to be found, I think, in the parallel that he sensed between the elemental nature of the Terror and the release of powerful instinctive forces that the writing of the book represented for him, which were far too native to him to be repudiated, and yet of which he was deeply afraid. No adequate reading of *The French Revolution* can neglect this level of interpretation entirely. Moreover, it casts light on what was to become one of the central issues of Carlyle's later writings – his attitude to democracy.

Carlyle was never a democrat. He sympathised deeply with the poor, but he had no faith in the Chartists' panacea of the ballot box as their remedy; he was equally contemptuous of the relatively liberal French constitution of 1791 and the relatively democratic one of 1793, seeing both as mere paper formulas with no relevance to the social and political realities of France at the time. But if he was no democrat, he had the Romantic's preference for instinct over reason; and the crowd could very easily become the symbol of the blind but irresistible instinct pitted against the conscious but fragile reason of the established order. The symbolism is apparent in his account of the storming of the Bastille:

Hast thou considered how each man's heart is so tremulously responsive to the hearts of all men; hast thou noted how omnipotent is the very sound of many men? How their shriek of indignation palsies the strong soul; their howl of contumely withers with unfelt pangs? The Ritter Gluck confessed that the ground-tone of the noblest passage, in one of his noblest Operas, was the voice of the Populace he had heard at Vienna, crying to their Kaiser: Bread! Bread! Great is the combined voice of men; the utterance of their *instincts*, which are truer than their *thoughts* . . . (R I 194).

In *The French Revolution* Carlyle was still on the side of the instincts, as against the repressive thoughts, though he was not to remain so much longer; the crowd, accordingly, is still seen as a creative force, though a blind and frightening one, not merely an object for the repressive will of the Hero. There is a curious passage in which Carlyle laments the decline of spontaneity in battles:

Battles, in these ages, are transacted by mechanism; with the slightest possible development of human individuality or spontaneity: men now even die, and kill one another, in an artificial manner. Battles ever since Homer's time, when they were Fighting Mobs, have mostly ceased to be worth looking at, worth reading of or remembering. (R I 251)

Although it is true that his account of the Revolution ends with Napoleon's famous 'whiff of grapeshot' on the 13th of Vendemiaire in 1795, there is no suggestion that this represents the glorious victory of reason over instinct, or of authority over insurrection: the explanation given is that the instincts have had full expression, and have worked themselves out. In that sense only, the time of order has come again.

It is certainly a mistake to see in *The French Revolution* nothing more than a tract for the times. But the importance of this element was greatly reinforced retrospectively by the fact that it foreshadowed the direction that Carlyle's thinking was to take for the next decade, and the role of social prophet with which he was to be above all associated. We have seen that a degree of concern with the condition of society can be traced at least as

far back as his visit to London in 1831–2, and on a more abstract level to his essay on 'Signs of the Times' of 1829. But in
the late 1830s this concern became increasingly his chief preoc-
cupation, and remained so throughout the following decade.
There is no difficulty in explaining this development, for it did
no more than mirror the public mood of the time; it was because his writings articulated that mood so pungently and
penetratingly that the 1840s brought Carlyle to the peak of his
public prestige and intellectual influence.

In 1837 a sharp downturn in the economy ushered in what
has come to be regarded as the most serious social crisis of the
nineteenth century in Britain. By this time, the Utopian expectations nurtured by the passing of the Reform Act had long
since foundered in disillusionment. The working class bitterly
resented what they regarded as their betrayal by the Whigs and
the middle class, who had used the threat of popular violence to
extort the Reform Act from the ruling aristocracy and had then
recompensed their erstwhile allies with the wholly inadequate
Factory Act of 1833, the persecution of the Tolpuddle Martyrs,
and above all the repressive New Poor Law of 1834. When the
depression of 1837 added industrial unemployment on a huge
scale to these grievances, the working class responded with the
Chartist movement, based on a demand for universal manhood
suffrage to be enforced by the weight of mass petitioning, and
rising to its first and probably most explosive crisis in the summer and autumn of 1839.

It was in the atmosphere of rising public alarm engendered
by these events that *The French Revolution* made its impact and
Carlyle's own attention came to be increasingly taken up with
the social crisis. Some indication of this can be seen in the
topics of the four successive annual courses of lectures that he
delivered in London between 1837 and 1840, for whereas the
first two were on the history of literature, and harked back to
his work for the Reviews in the 1820s, the last two, on the
revolutions of modern Europe and on 'Heroes and Hero-
Worship' (the only one of the four series to be published), were
both concerned with the real or ideal condition of society. But
these lectures were never more to Carlyle than an irksome
means of making ends meet. His mood of the time is much

better reflected in the long pamphlet with the significant title of *Chartism*, published in December 1839.

*Chartism* has received much less attention than it deserves. It has some claim to be considered the best piece of social criticism that Carlyle ever wrote (though his characteristic weaknesses are also to be discerned in it), and it anticipates the major themes of all his later writings in the field, as well as coining two famous phrases, 'the Condition of England Question' and 'the cash nexus', which were to become commonplaces of social debate throughout the next decade. In spite of its title, the Chartist movement itself is not the major theme of the pamphlet; it is only the latest and most alarming manifestation of the 'deep-lying struggle in the whole fabric of society' that he had already identified in 'Signs of the Times' ten years before. Nor had Carlyle any sympathy with the Chartist remedy, universal manhood suffrage. The pursuit of the franchise had always been a pursuit of the will-o'-the-wisp, and the record of the reformed Parliament since 1832 gave him no reason whatever to think that a more representative Parliament would cure the social evils of the time. The importance of Chartism to him was the self-evident fact that it bespoke a depth of human suffering which insistently and irresistibly demanded action. This theme, already emphasised in the first book of *The French Revolution*, emerges in *Chartism* as the central element in the indictment of contemporary British society – that suffering on this scale is the fault of the ruling class of the society which permits it. It is in connection with the appalling poverty of Ireland under English rule (a problem which attracted a great deal of Carlyle's attention over the next ten years) that he makes the point most trenchantly:

> Ireland has near seven millions of working people, the third unit of whom, it appears by Statistic Science, has not for thirty weeks each year as many third-rate potatoes as will suffice him. It is a fact perhaps the most eloquent that was ever written down in any language, at any date of the world's history ... A government and guidance of white European men which has issued in perennial hunger of potatoes to the third man extant, – ought to drop a veil over its face, and walk out of

court under conduct of proper officers; saying no word; ex-
cepting now of a surety sentence either to change or to die . . .
England is guilty towards Ireland; and reaps at last, in full
measure, the fruit of fifteen generations of wrong-doing.
(E IV 136)

The proclamation of England's guilt at the end of this passage is an excellent example of the sort of trenchant statement
of plain but heretical moral truth that many of the keener minds
of the younger generation found most attractive in Carlyle's social criticism of this period. Equally interesting is the last sentence, for it illustrates the way in which Carlyle typically saw
providential justice working itself out in history. English mis-
government had brought starvation in Ireland. The consequence was the arrival in England in the 1830s and 1840s of an
accelerating flood of poverty-stricken Irish labourers, unable to
survive in their own country, whose competition undercut
wages in England and created unemployment, in turn leading to
the rise of mass popular discontent in the form of Chartism. In
this way, Carlyle argues, the chickens of aristocratic neglect
finally come home to roost. The fiercest denunciations in *Chartism* are reserved for the *laissez-faire* theorists who deny on
dogmatic grounds that there is anything the state can do to re-
lieve suffering; an attitude which Carlyle stigmatises as 'Paraly-
tic Radicalism' and dismisses memorably with the aphorism
that 'the public highways ought not to be occupied by people
demonstrating that motion is impossible'. Twentieth-century
developments may be thought to give that remark a wry or ominous look; but in the context of Britain in the 1830s it had to
contemporaries a keen point, and it clearly looks forward to the
more generalised indictment of the 'Dilettante Aristocracy' in
*Past and Present* four years later.

Within this indictment of inertia on the part of the ruling class
there lies an important implication which was to have great influence on the future development of Carlyle's thinking and of his
public reputation – an implication that is already clearly drawn
out in *Chartism*, though at far less length than in *Past and Present*. To Carlyle, the ruling class of a society is responsible for the
moral and physical well-being of the people over whom it rules;

but it is responsible for the people rather than to them. The responsibility is upward, to the divine justice that presides over the social order. It is true that it is part of the machinery of that divine justice that, as in the case of Ireland, an élite that neglects its responsibilities will find itself confronted with a Chartist movement, or, worse, a French Revolution. But this is the last resort; the duty of a ruling class is not to carry out the will of the people, but to rule them. This does not imply a crude despotism or oligarchy, though these possibilities were already latent within Carlyle's ideas, and were to become steadily more prominent in it in later years. The true relation between rulers and ruled is complex and mutually dependent. In a healthy society, the ruler is recognised by the ruled as their natural leader, almost as their emanation; a sense of mutual responsibility binds them together. 'Surely of all "rights of man"', Carlyle says, 'this right of the ignorant man to be guided by the wiser . . . is the indisputablest . . . If Freedom have any meaning, it means enjoyment of this right, wherein all other rights are enjoyed. It is a sacred right and duty, on both sides; and the summation of all social duties whatsoever between the two' (E IV 157–8). The worst corruption of contemporary British society lies in the denial of this right and duty. In *Chartism* Carlyle sees this denial as the fault of the rulers not the ruled: the Chartist movement is to him the inarticulate protest of the ruled against the failure of guidance from above. He found the origin of this failure in the contemporary domination of the public conscience by the utilitarian frame of mind derived from the teachings of Jeremy Bentham. This was his old bogey, the philosophy of the Enlightenment that he had had to fight against so hard in his student days at Edinburgh, in a new form; a form that sought to reduce human emotions to measurable quantities, human relationships to mechanical interactions, human dealings to sheer calculations of profit and loss. The only bond left between men was the 'cash nexus', the mere buying and selling of services for money, all broader responsibilities and loyalties being denied in a reduction ultimately intolerable to human nature. The idea of the cash nexus is only sketched in *Chartism*; but it was to have a brilliant ideological future before it, and has been made the basis of what is perhaps still the most serious moral indictment of capitalism.

By his position on this issue, Carlyle made completely clear for the first time the unbridgeable chasm that separated his ideas from the democratic forms of radicalism. He had widely been regarded as an extreme radical, and almost all his previous writings had appeared in Whig or Radical periodicals. *Chartism* for the first time led some to regard him as a Tory, and indeed Carlyle hesitated long over whether it should appear in the Radical *Westminster Review* or the Tory *Quarterly Review*, and finally decided to publish it separately. Carlyle never regarded himself as anything but a radical: 'The people are beginning to discover that I am not a Tory', he wrote approvingly a few weeks after the book's publication. 'Ah, no! but one of the deepest, though perhaps the quietest, of all the Radicals now extant in the world' (N I 185); and for a decade or more after 1839 he continued to be generally accepted at this valuation, on the strength of his undoubted dedication to social (as distinct from political) reform, and the vehemence of his criticism of existing society. Up to this time, of course, experience seemed to most observers to confirm his view of democracy as a wildly unpractical political system; and Carlyle was a realist who hated cant and dogmatism and insisted that the first quality required of an idea was that it should be able to stand up to the test of practice. Democracy to him was a Utopian creed which had failed in the French Revolution because of its neglect of the realities of power; its proponents, the Girondins, had gone down before the Jacobins, who knew and respected those realities; and it would always fail for the same reasons.

The essentially mystical feeling for the processes of history that Carlyle shared with Hegel, Marx and other great thinkers of the nineteenth century necessarily involves the thinker in the baffling dialectic of might and right; and in *Chartism* this issue, which was to perplex Carlyle for the rest of his life and to become the ground of many indictments of his work, first comes to the surface. His position is far from clear. Like many others, he shrank from the crudity of saying that might makes right, but found himself driven towards that position by the logic of his thinking. He says at one time that no system and no outcome can last without general acceptance, and that it can only win acceptance if it satisfies men's sense of right, which may be true, and is certainly morally acceptable; but he also says that the pursuit of wholly impracticable rights (which might include democracy) is a misuse of time and effort, which may also be true but is far less morally acceptable, since it amounts to saying that might confines right, even if it does not define it.

It is typical of the weakness of Carlyle as a systematic thinker that he makes no real attempt in *Chartism* to identify the causes of the suffering to which he calls attention, and that the concrete remedies that he suggests are manifestly inadequate for a crisis of the proportions that he has described. For causes, he is content to look no further than to lack of leadership on the part of the governing class, which is obviously too diffuse an explanation to be satisfactory. Carlyle was aware of the Malthusian explanation – over-population – and has some admirably pungent comments on the proposed Malthusian remedies, but he attempts no estimate of the validity of the explanation itself. The most obvious alternative explanation of the crisis was to view it as a consequence of the rapid growth of industrialisation; but this too is a hypothesis that Carlyle hardly considers. Carlyle is simply not an analytical thinker. A passage from *The French Revolution* is very much to the point: 'But to gauge and measure this immeasurable Thing, and what is called *account for it*, and reduce it to a dead logic-formula, attempt not!... As an actually existing Son of Time, *look*, with unspeakable manifold interest, oftenest in silence, at what the Time did bring: therewith edify, instruct, nourish thyself...' (R I 213). Carlyle's concern in *Chartism*, as in *The French Revolution*, is not to account for the phenomenon he describes, but to force his reader into the 'bodily, concrete, coloured presence' of it, and to compel him to a moral response. The assumption is fundamental to Carlyle that the moral response is everything; once it is made, intellectual solutions will present themselves.

It is not that Carlyle was unaware of the importance of the transformation being wrought in British society by the impact of industrialisation; on the contrary, he probably had a profounder awareness of it than any other contemporary critic. But, like D. H. Lawrence's reaction to the same phenomenon almost a century later, it was an awareness primarily of the im-

agination rather than of the intellect; and it was too profound to
reduce the Industrial Revolution to nothing more than a cause
of social distress, for Carlyle had an equally acute apprehension
of the grandly creative aspect of industrialisation. He was aware
of the lot of the handloom weavers and the factory children –
we have seen how he twisted his account of the Dauphin's fate
in *The French Revolution* to draw attention to it – and yet at the
same time he can write a finely poetic passage in *Chartism* on
the grandeur of the sound of the Manchester cotton-mills starting up at half-past five in the morning 'like the boom of an
Atlantic tide', and balance the creativity against the evil: 'Cot-
ton-spinning is the clothing of the naked in its result; the
triumph of man over matter in its means. Soot and despair are
not the essence of it; they are divisible from it' (E IV 182). There
is nothing better in Carlyle's social criticism than this tension,
his ability to see the good and the evil simultaneously and with
equal vividness, and without attempting any easy trade-off between them. It was a tension sustained only with difficulty and
at great inner cost, and Carlyle would not sustain it indefinitely.

As to Carlyle's prescriptions for the crisis, his whole emphasis
falls once more on the necessity of responsible leadership. In a
long rhapsodic chapter, he invokes the two thousand years of
the nation's past as a record of creative achievement, from the
first landing of the Saxons and the clearing of the land for cul-
tivation, to the achievements of Shakespeare and Milton in literature and of Arkwright and Watt in industry. The implication
is that a similar creative effort is required to deal with the existing social crisis; but at the moment none is forthcoming:
'Where now are the Hengsts and Alarics of our still-glowing,
still-expanding Europe? . . . Preserving their game!' (E IV 204).
In this passage, repeated from *Sartor Resartus*, Carlyle returns,
as he often does, to the Game Laws (which reserved all game,
even including rabbits, for the landlord) as the symbol of a ruling class which sacrifices the well-being of its inferiors to its
own idle pleasures. He makes only two concrete proposals for
dealing with the social crisis – emigration and education.
Emigration was much in Carlyle's mind at this time, as we have
seen; and among those who saw the social problem as primarily
a matter of over-population it was a fashionable nostrum in the

1840s. But, as some critics said at the time, education and emigration could not by themselves possibly be adequate solutions for the crisis. Carlyle would probably not have denied it; indeed in *Chartism* itself he satirises the emigrationists. But it was above all a moral response that he was trying to evoke; and without this, any specific proposals could easily become mere formulas as hollow as franchise reform had proved to be. Nevertheless, the weakness is undoubtedly a real and serious one. One of the strengths of *Chartism* is that in it Carlyle made his most determined attempt to wed the force of his moral vision to the empiricism of counted and measured facts. He does, for instance, argue powerfully and effectively that all estimates of the conditions of the working classes are totally inadequate in the absence of adequate statistical studies. But when it comes to suggesting remedies this empiricism is lacking; and the weakness mars a work which in other respects remains a most powerful and penetrating piece of social criticism, marking the increasing emergence of Carlyle in his new role of social prophet.

# 4 The prophetic role

By the early 1840s Carlyle was no longer a young man; and though his reputation was only just approaching its zenith, the most creative phase of his writing was already behind him. The main themes had already been stated, and the imaginative fire was beginning to cool. It is unlikely that any serious critic would want to put any of his writings after 1840, except *Past and Present*, into the same category as *Sartor Resartus* and *The French Revolution*; and all the major themes even of *Past and Present* had been anticipated in *Chartism*.

But it was between the publication of *The French Revolution* in 1837 and of *Latter Day Pamphlets* in 1850 that Carlyle's real influence, if not his public reputation, was at its height. With *The French Revolution*, one might say, he won the ear of a generation, and with the *Pamphlets* he lost it. During this span of a dozen years, his influence upon the rising intellectual generation was so extraordinary that it has never been approached in modern British history by any other single intellectual figure, not even by the great systematic thinkers such as Freud in the 1920s and Marx in the 1930s, with whom in their own field Carlyle could not stand serious comparison. The dominance is the more remarkable in that it was above all the young, the intelligent and the original who felt most strongly the impact of Carlyle's personality and the force of his ideas; and the spectrum of opinion that they represented ranged all the way from the utilitarian radical John Stuart Mill to the Coleridgean John Sterling (and even on to Tories like Southey and Lockhart). It was in these years that one of the most remarkable intellectual coteries in British literary history was established around the Carlyles' modest home in Cheyne Row. As Thackeray once said, 'Tom Carlyle lives in perfect dignity in a little house in Chelsea, with a snuffy Scotch maid to open the door, and the best company in England ringing at it.' The roll of his friends and disciples in the early 1840s is astonishing: Mill (though this remarkable friendship was already past its peak by 1840), his fellow radical Charles Buller, the indefatigable publicist and populariser Harriet Martineau, the brilliant and versatile John Sterling, son of the editor of *The Times*, novelists like Thackeray, Dickens and Elizabeth Gaskell, poets like Browning, Tennyson and Edward Fitzgerald (the translator of *Omar Khayyam*), public figures like Charles Kingsley and Thomas Arnold, prominent political refugees from the Continent like Giuseppe Mazzini and Godefroi Cavaignac – all fell, to varying degrees, under Carlyle's spell. Most of them, moreover, came to him rather than he to them, and they came above all, to judge by most accounts of these visits, to hear him talk. In this sense, 'coterie' is perhaps the wrong word; this was not a club of wits, nor a literary discussion group. It was more like the gatherings at the Mitre to hear Johnson talk; yet Johnson was as much a performer as a teacher, and his listeners came less to learn than for the pleasure of witnessing the 'tossing and goring' of his interlocutors. The style of the visitors to Cheyne Row, and of the increasingly eager and numerous circle of Carlyle's readers in the 1840s, was different: it was the style of disciples about a prophet.

As soon as one tries to define Carlyle's role and the nature of his unique influence in the Britain of the 1840s, this word can never be kept out of the discussion for long: it was repeatedly used by his contemporaries themselves. What are the implications of the term? The prophet is an outsider, a moralist, a proclaimer, a messenger who recalls an erring society to the true path. He is not primarily a thinker, and most certainly not an analytical thinker. His authority is *ex cathedra*, and this is reflected in the tone of his pronouncements. He is also not primarily a predictor (though often incidentally one), for he offers a choice, a chance of repentance and redemption (the use of Biblical language is inevitable, for it is in the Bible that the role is defined); the historical schematists, such as Toynbee and Marx, are not prophets (though admittedly Marx's moral fervour does tend to obscure the distinction). The prophetic role, moreover, is ephemeral, and symbiotic. Because the prophet speaks with great intensity to the particular needs of a single society and a single generation, it is unlikely that his message can retain its relevance and appeal, as a great work of art or a great system of thought can; and, although the prophet is an outsider to his society and a denouncer of it, in the style of John the Baptist and Elijah, it is also true that without that society as an audience, the role is unimaginable. Unlike the artist or thinker, the prophet wholly unrecognised by his own generation is a contradiction in terms.

Carlyle's background, earlier life, and talents fitted him well for the role. In both national and social terms he was an outsider to respectable English society (he retained his broad Annandale accent, as well as his local Annandale loyalties, all his life), which was a brilliant advantage for the prophetic role. Not that this was a conscious strategy on Carlyle's part, for he was a man of transparent simplicity and integrity of character who would have been incapable of such a thing; rather, he became the great Victorian prophet because that was what his qualities made him. Carlyle never ceased to be the wild man from the hills; and whereas for a purely literary figure like Burns, whose background was very similar to Carlyle's, outsidership was a disaster (as Carlyle himself, obviously very sensible to the parallel to his own position, argues in his essay on Burns), it made Carlyle as a prophet a far more convincing spokesman of the quasi-divine message of condemnation and call to repentance. The nineteenth century was a great age of prophets, but the impact of the message of men like Ruskin and Morris was to some extent blunted by the fact that they were insiders to their society. Carlyle alone, as the wild Scot and working man's son, could speak with the authority of the true prophet.

The prophetic role was of course familiar to Carlyle from the strongly Biblical and Calvinist background of his childhood; and the experience of spiritual isolation at Edinburgh University, and of the long rejection of his writings, gave him the sense of apartness essential to it. What he still needed was the prophetic message; and this first came to him in the form of German Romanticism. After that he had an ample intellectual platform from which to denounce the intellectual sterilities of the eighteenth century. The voice of the prophet is already clearly audible in his review articles of the 1820s announcing the new German gospel to the British public; but so far the message was largely confined to the literary, and wholly to the intellectual, sphere. It was its translation into social terms, closely linked with his move to London in the early 1830s, that completed Carlyle's emergence by the end of the decade as the prophet of modern British society. It is very noticeable, in this connection, how rapidly Carlyle's mental development in the 1830s led him away from German Romanticism. Certainly he never abjured it; he retained his personal admiration for its heroes, and for all things German, to the end of his life. But already by 1837 he could describe himself as 'far parted now' from Goethe, once the lodestar of his existence. References to German literature are sparse in both his books and his correspondence after 1834, and after his bread-and-butter lectures on the topic in 1837, he turned away from it for good. Though transformed by his encounter with Germany, it was the world of ideas of the Old Testament imbibed in Annandale in his childhood, that increasingly dominated his thinking in the 1830s and 1840s; and this of course was the world of the prophets. As early as 1833 he was writing to Mill 'Not in Poetry, but only if so might be in Prophecy, in stern old-Hebrew denunciation, can one speak of the accursed realities that now, and for generations . . . weigh heavy on us!' (T VI 370).

Carlyle's temperament and the nature of his talents exactly suited him for the prophetic role. He was a man at one and the same time of great warmth and spontaneity and of austere and formidable force of character. Though he was not a systematic thinker, he had a brilliantly imaginative and strikingly original mind. He could talk freely as an equal with his friends. His best friend at this time, John Sterling, disagreed with him often and vehemently, and in a memorable phrase Carlyle described their walks together round Chelsea: 'arguing copiously, but *except* in opinion not disagreeing' (J 106). But open-minded discussion could never be easy for a man who held his opinions as passionately as Carlyle did, and increasingly with the years his tendency was toward an authoritarian habit of speech which would brook no denial – the natural dialect of a prophet, all the more when linked with a vocabulary and a flow of images as vivid and arresting as Carlyle's. This, and the intensity of moral conviction that accompanied it, is well illustrated in an anecdote related by his friend Emerson, who once bravely declared his inability to go all the way with Carlyle's enthusiasm for Oliver Cromwell: Carlyle 'rose like a great Norse giant from his chair – and, drawing a line with his finger across the table, said, with terrible fierceness: Then, sir, there is a line of separation between you and me as wide as that, and as deep as the pit.' A man of these qualities, together with a completely unpretentious personal life of great simplicity, had all the makings of a prophet.

But the prophetic symbiosis requires a properly endowed audience as well as a properly endowed speaker; and in the early 1840s there existed in England an audience superbly equipped to listen to what Carlyle had to say. It should be said at once that this was an audience predominantly limited to the educated classes. Carlyle never repudiated or disguised his own working-class background, nor lost his reverence for the working man. Some working men read his work; some few even wrote to him, and were answered as readily and as helpfully as any of his many correspondents. Nevertheless all his writings from the beginning were addressed to the educated public; and it was among them that the prophet found his fit audience. Given Carlyle's emphasis on conscientious leadership as the prime necessity for society, it made sense that he should address himself to the ruling classes of his country; and his message spoke directly to the peculiar needs of that single generation of that class.

It was a generation that still sought answers to its problems in religious forms, but which at the same time found the traditional religious formulas unsatisfying. The reasons for this include the rationalist scepticism of the eighteenth century, the development of Biblical criticism and of scientific geology – both throwing doubt on the literal truth of the Bible – and the failure of the Churches to respond adequately to the growing social crisis. The spirited counter-offensives mounted by the Churches in the first half of the century in the face of these challenges – Methodism, Evangelicalism, the Oxford Movement, the Roman Catholic revival – failed to satisfy many of the best minds of the rising generation; and a great many of them found relief in Carlyle's outspoken denunciation of the Churches as mere hollow shells of what had once been authentic symbols of the divine

instinct in men. Yet Carlyle did not leave his readers in the
scepticism which for most men of the 1840s was still an intellectually unbreathable atmosphere. He held out to them the prospect of a new kind of faith, to be obtained as the prize of a
pilgrimage as rigorous as Teufelsdrockh's in *Sartor Resartus*. It
was a faith never very precisely defined, an amalgam of German
Idealism and a rigorously moralistic and providential system of
values derived from the Old Testament; but in the short run at
least the lack of definition was an asset, the one aspect appealing
to the generation's typical Romanticism as much as the other
appealed to its inherited Christian values. Not only did Carlyle
offer a *believable* alternative to traditional Christianity; he
offered one with its roots deep in the real world and with its
own divinely-inspired Scripture in the supernatural justice that
governed the course of history. He also offered a creed which
had all the emotional and moral colour and challenge that the
most formidable alternative non-Christian intellectual system
available in Britain at the time, Utilitarianism, conspicuously
lacked, and which the young instinctively demanded. The intellectual foundations, and the precise content, of the Carlylean
morality might admit of some doubt; of its overwhelming
earnestness there was no doubt whatever. One of the most ardent of Carlyle's disciples, his great biographer James Anthony
Froude, who first came before the public as the author of the
sceptical *succès de scandale* entitled *The Nemesis of Faith*, summed up Carlyle's influence on his generation thus:

I, for one, was saved by Carlyle's writings from Positivism,
or Romanism, or Atheism, or any other of the creeds or no
creeds which in those years were whirling us about in Oxford
like leaves in an autumn storm. The controversies of the
place had unsettled the faith which we had inherited. The
alternatives were being thrust upon us of believing nothing,
or believing everything which superstition, disguised as
Church authority, had been pleased to impose; or, as a third
course, and a worse one, of acquiescing, for worldly conveni-
ence, in the established order of things, which had been made
intellectually incredible. Carlyle taught me a creed which I
could then accept as really true; which I have held ever since,

with increasing confidence, as the interpretation of my existence and the guide of my conduct, so far as I have been able
to act up to it. (F I 295–6)

But this accounts only for the less important part of Carlyle's
impact on early Victorian England. The prophet is a messenger to
society, not merely to the individual. Carlyle was a preacher of
*social* sin and salvation, and in this respect too the message fell
on ears exceptionally well tuned to receive it. The British public
conscience was in a peculiarly sensitive condition in the years
before 1848. On the one hand there were the recurrent rumbles
of revolution from the Continent – principally the French revolutions of 1789 and 1830 – to point the Carlylean moral of
what happened to erring societies and frivolous and irrespon-
sible ruling classes; and the social unrest of 1815–20 and the
Reform Bill crisis of 1831–2 had done much to make revolution
imaginable in Britain also. In addition, there was growing uneasiness about the uncontrolled and traumatic social changes
sweeping over Britain as a consequence of industrialisation –
urbanisation, poverty in both cities and countryside, and
large-scale periodic unemployment among the most serious of
them. In the relatively prosperous years of the mid-1830s it had
been possible to believe the optimistic pronouncements of *laissez-faire* economists that these were only teething troubles; but
the renewed plunge into ever deeper and more frightening
depths of depression after 1837, accompanied by the revival of
mass working-class discontent, lent support to the view that the
new economic system contained insoluble built-in weaknesses,
and convinced many that the moment of reckoning might indeed be approaching. There was also the sheer sense of insecur-
ity bred of living in an age of rapid and quite unparalleled social
and economic change.

It was just at this time, in the late 1830s and early 1840s, that
the first large-scale objective inquiries into the working and living conditions of the poorer classes were taking place in Britain,
with the Report of the Select Committee on the Labour of Children in Factories in 1832 at one end, and Henry Mayhew's
famous articles on 'London Labour and the London Poor' in
1849–52 at the other. During these years a succession of Par-

liamentary Committees and Royal Commissions, backed by the
new Poor Law Commission established in 1834, issued a series
of massive reports which for the first time made available exact
evidence on what life was like for the poor, especially the urban
poor, in the new industrial England. Independent inquirers
added their own reports of their findings on their tours of the
industrial north; the prominence of what, following Carlyle's
cue, came to be widely known as 'The Condition of England
Question' was reflected too in the extensive debates of the issues
in the pages of the great Reviews, in cartoons, and in the growing vogue of the 'social novel', the model set by Disraeli's *Sybil*
in 1845. The campaigns of the Anti-Corn Law League, the
three successive crises of the Chartist movement in 1839, 1842
and 1848, and the appalling famine that struck Ireland in the
wake of the potato blight of 1845–6 gave immediate and most
urgent topical point to the issues.

It was an age when *The Times* was in the forefront of the
onslaught on the inhumanities of the New Poor Law, and when
even *Punch* could be radical; a period of deep social introver-
sion, when the mind of the educated British public was turned
in on the state of British society more profoundly, and with an
acuter sense of moral uneasiness, than it has ever been since. At
various times there was also widespread fear. But fear was not
the dominant emotion in most of the discussions of the problem. In the main the issues were faced with a moral seriousness
and an intellectual open-mindedness which did much credit to
the British society of that generation, whatever may be thought
of the conclusions reached.

An educated society so conscious of social evils, so anxious
for guidance in tackling them, and so unusually ready to con-
template novel and unorthodox solutions, was an audience
ready-made for a prophet. In Carlyle the man was at hand – the
only man with a message whose scale and radicalism seemed to
meet the scale of the problem, and about whose personality
there hung the genuine prophetic aura; a man who seemed to be
able to envisage the kind of total moral regeneration of society
which alone seemed adequate to the scale of the crisis. Increasingly in the years after 1837 Carlyle found that the winds
of public opinion, which had blown obstinately against him for

so long, were shifting in his favour. His books began to sell; his lectures were eagerly attended; he had the ear of the younger generation, with his message of social apocalypse and social re-generation. What use he was to make of this position remained to be seen.

# 5 The prophetic decade

The direction of Carlyle's thinking in the years after the publication of *The French Revolution* was somewhat confused. We have seen that the publication of *Chartism* in 1839 marked unmistakably the coming of the social issue to the forefront of his mind, in close relationship with the deepening of the economic crisis. There followed the publication of *Heroes and Hero-Worship* in 1840. But this was no more than the fourth of the annual series of lectures that Carlyle had undertaken in London, originally out of pure bread-and-butter motives; the fact that it was the only one of the four to be published by Carlyle may have given it undue prominence, and show only that by 1840 publishers were eager for his custom. Nevertheless, hero-worship was to be an increasingly prominent, and ultimately dominant, theme in all Carlyle's later writing. It was not new in 1840. It can be traced back through all Carlyle's writings to its original source in Fichte; but it is in *Heroes and Hero-Worship* that it comes fully into the open as the central feature of Carlyle's view of society. The 'Hero' is the messenger of the divine to the mass of mankind who cannot hear its injunctions for themselves; he is, in fact, in a broad sense the prophet. The prophet can, however, appear in a variety of roles; in *Heroes and Hero-Worship* Carlyle singles out six: the divinity, the prophet, the poet, the priest, the man of letters and the king. The Protean nature of the hero here is worth noting. Carlyle had first seen the hero as man of letters (clearly the role that had most relevance to his own condition), and in his later writings he was to be almost exclusively the king. But in 1840 the conception was still fairly plastic; and it is characteristic of most of the heroes Carlyle chooses to illustrate his theme that they rise to heroism from obscurity; they are, so to speak, meritocratic heroes. The spirit blows whither it listeth. A healthy society is defined by its ability to recognise its heroes and its readiness to listen to them; and since they may come from anywhere, a relatively fluid society is likely to be best adapted for the purpose.

The great virtue of revolutions is that they provide this fluidity. They allow the true heroes of a society, the Cromwells, the Mirabeaus, the Napoleons, to rise to the top. It is significant that in his lecture on 'The Hero as King' Carlyle's two chief exemplars are Cromwell and Napoleon, and no hereditary monarchs at all.

In retrospect, *Heroes and Hero-Worship* has no place with Carlyle's best work. It was not directly related to the contemporary crisis in British society, and to Carlyle himself it was something of a distraction from the main task that he had increasingly in mind, a history of the Puritan revolution of the seventeenth century in England. Yet it cannot be neglected, for hero-worship was to be a central theme in all Carlyle's later work, and in the view of most of his critics, a distorting one. *Heroes and Hero-Worship* was to be one of the most popular of Carlyle's books, yet the reiteration of its theme was ultimately to be largely responsible for alienating many of Carlyle's ablest and most ardent disciples of the 1840s. The popularity of the book may be accounted for by the fact that it demanded of its readers a readiness neither to tolerate an aggressive novelty of literary style and form, as *Sartor* had done, nor to master a mass of historical detail, nor to face up to the implications of a searching moral critique of contemporary society. An unkind critic might indeed say that it required little but a susceptibility to vague moral uplift; but this is too harsh. Inexactly formulated though it may be, there is a serious content to Carlyle's idea of hero-worship, and even if one regards it as tangential or irrelevant to what was most valuable in his thinking, it remains to be explained why to Carlyle himself it took on such importance.

Carlyle was never a democrat. Given his social background and talents, this is surprising; his radicalism could have taken a democratic turn, though whether this would have made him more or less effective as a prophet is hard to say. He would have won less upper-class patronage from the early 1840s onward, but he might have retained the more valuable allegiance of the Mills and the Cloughs, and might of course also have made a strong appeal to a working-class readership, and given the Chartist movement the authentic prophetic voice that it never found for itself. But he had an element of tough realism in him at a time

when most contemporaries saw democracy as a wholly un-
realistic creed. Moreover the strong strain of élitism in the German Romantic thinkers had had a deep influence on his intellectual development. To Carlyle democracy was the offspring of
the Enlightenment, and this alone was enough to condemn it.
Carlyle was no political theorist, and if he ever read Burke it is
not apparent in his writings. Yet his picture of the good society,
as it dimly emerges in *Chartism*, in *Past and Present* and in *Oliver Cromwell*, has much in common with the organic, closely in-
tegrated, hierarchical society that Burke envisages in its un-
forced unity of sentiment, its rejection of the seductive claims of
abstract Reason, its religious faith and its willing acceptance of
leadership from above. But here the one divergence between
them arises. Burke has no theory of hero-worship; for him, leadership comes from the traditional ruling class, the landed aristocracy, and is accepted as natural with an unquestioning seren-
ity which is far remote from the note of high-flown romanticism
and even hysteria implicit in such a term as 'hero-worship'.
Why the difference?

By 1840, the date of *Heroes and Hero-Worship*, it was no longer possible for any sensitive observer to locate authority in the
traditional landed aristocracy with the same composure as
Burke. Even so, the explanation of Carlyle's view probably lies
more in his personal position in society. As an archetypal
'loner', who had made his own the essentially solitary role of
prophet, he had not made his way in life (as Burke did) by
associating himself with the efforts of any social class or group
to enlarge its powers or its liberties. The image of the working
man's son was useful for the outsider's stance it gave him in
addressing polite society; but he never worked closely *with*
working men, and was essentially a member of that most anar-
chic of all sects, the literary intellectuals. He had made his way
in the face of daunting difficulties purely by his own talents and
efforts; and the position he had achieved was not merely a de-
cent footing in English upper-class society, but that of the
prophetic proclaimer of truth to peasant and peer alike. This
was a heroic role, and required a theory of hero-worship to sustain it; and the form of society in which it might flourish could
not be a democratic one, for it assumed the ready recognition of

authority originating, not in mandate from below, but in commission from above. Carlyle's cult of the hero and rejection of democracy are likely to strike a twentieth-century reader as unsympathetic; but seen against the background of his time, circumstances and personality, it is possible to understand them.

That Carlyle should turn after 1839 to the Puritan revolution as the subject next demanding his attention is not surprising. This was a theme which had interested him intermittently since the early 1820s, and it was entirely congenial to him, echoing as it did the Puritanism of his own family background and Scottish national history. To him the Puritan revolution ranked with the Reformation and the French Revolution as the grand theodicies of modern history – in the language of Idealism, the breakthrough of the Real into the world of shams; in the language of the Old Testament, the sentence of Providence on a corrupt society. Here was the subject for a book, and in 1840 he set to work on it; but it was never to be written in this form. He could not shape the material as he wished, in spite of months of the agonising labour that literary composition almost always entailed for him; and in any case his mind was increasingly taken up with the mounting tide of social distress around him. In the grim winter of 1841–2, in a typically sharp piece of social observation, he had noticed for the first time garden palings in Chelsea torn up and stolen for fuel: 'a bitter symptom, for the people in general are very honest' (A 535); and in the autumn of 1842, on a tour of the eastern counties to gather material for his history, he saw in passing the crowd of unemployed in St Ives workhouse in Huntingdonshire, which was to provide him with the opening scene for *Past and Present*. The crisis seemed to call for an utterance from him, and he abandoned work on his history for this more urgent task; this time the book flowed easily, and *Past and Present* was published in April 1843.

This event marks the peak of Carlyle's prophetic career. His correspondence clearly reflects the closeness of the interest that he was taking in the problems of society at this time, and in issues such as the Poor Law, the campaign for the repeal of the Corn Laws (a campaign with which he strongly sympathised, but in which he refused to become personally involved), and the condition of Ireland. *Past and Present* was in some ways the fullest and weightiest of all Carlyle's social pronouncements; and it came at the moment when the public ear was uniquely well prepared to receive it. It has always been regarded as one of his major works, not least because of the inspiration it gave to later social critics as diverse as Friedrich Engels and John Ruskin. It is, with two exceptions, essentially a fuller, more carefully worked out version of *Chartism*, and one which achieved much wider currency because its audience was much better prepared. Its starting point is the fact of mass hardship, and the moral responsibility that this places upon the ruling classes of the country, who bear the guilt for the suffering; in the same way, in *Chartism*, Carlyle had proclaimed their guilt toward Ireland. The vivid description in the first chapter of the unemployed that Carlyle had seen in the St Ives workhouse a few months before ushers in this theme. In the years since he wrote *Chartism*, the novel and little-understood phenomenon of mass industrial unemployment had increased to a huge extent, and outbreaks of rioting in the industrial north in the summer of 1842 seemed to hold out the threat of revolutionary violence – a scenario straight out of Carlyle's *French Revolution*. Carlyle effectively brings out the irony of the gigantic productive possibilities unleashed by the Industrial Revolution set against the unemployment that had resulted from it, and the moral anomaly of men willing and anxious to work who yet cannot find work. But there is no attempt at any analysis of the economics of the problem. Carlyle never showed any interest in economics, which to him always remained associated with the 'dismal science' and moral irresponsibility of *laissez-faire*; a blind spot on which the immense sophistication of economic thought since Carlyle's day has cast a harsh light, but which went little noticed at the time. His own analysis is again, as in *Chartism*, purely moral: unemployment is, in some way never precisely explained, the consequence of the reduction of what should be personal relationships to merely economic ones, of the denial of responsibility by the ruling classes; and it is only in the re-emergence of a ruling class that accepts its responsibility that a solution can lie. Once again Carlyle emphatically refuses to produce anything like a list of specific prescriptions for the crisis, since to do so would blunt the essentially moral nature of his

message. Once again there is reference to emigration and education, both to be organised and undertaken by the state. There is
even brief mention of the possibility of giving employees a
financial interest in their firm, the germ of the co-operative
principle which attracted a good deal of interest in the 1840s.
But the nearest approach to a practical programme is the demand for 'permanence of contract'. Having placed the blame
for the crisis upon the shifting and purely economic nature of
personal relationships under the new economic system, Carlyle
argued with some logic that the solution was to substitute a
system under which the relationship between master and man
should be permanent. The idea has some interest, and curiously
brings to mind one of the features of the Japanese economic
system which is often adduced to explain the superiority of the
Japanese economic performance in recent years; but Carlyle
once more shrinks away from explaining in any detail how such
a relationship might work, and indeed the examples he uses are
the less attractive ones of European feudalism and West Indian
slavery.

Yet for all its weaknesses, *Past and Present* is a tract for its
times of compelling power, by reason of the intensity of its moral
concern for the future of British society, and the depth and
sincerity of the sympathy for human suffering upon which it
unmistakably rests. Fear may have been one of the motives
which induced Carlyle's contemporaries to listen to his message
in the 1840s, but it was a motive from which Carlyle himself
was wholly free. Neither in *Past and Present* nor in *Chartism* is
there any hint of the rationalising tone, the attempt to defend
the privileged position of one's own social group, which infects
so much social criticism. The other great distinction of *Past
and Present* is its remarkable second book, 'The Ancient Monk',
the section which explains the word 'Past' in the title.

Book II is a description of life in the Abbey of Bury St
Edmund's in the late twelfth century. The idea for it arose from
a recent item of Carlyle's omnivorous historical reading, a new-
ly-published edition of a twelfth-century chronicle of life in the
Abbey by one of its monks, Jocelin of Brakelond. His chronicle
is, by any standards, a remarkable record of medieval monastic
life; but few men would have seen in it a stick with which to

beat the nineteenth century, which is what it became in Carlyle's hands. 'The Ancient Monk' is the finest example of the way in which, to Carlyle, history was never a merely academic study, but had a prophetic function to serve. Medievalism itself was of course a widespread intellectual fashion at the time, but to most of its adherents it was no more than a wistful nostalgia, a rejection of the present. To Carlyle it was a great deal more. Twelfth-century England becomes a model of the healthy society, not in its picturesque trappings, which are irretrievably of the past, but in its moral essence, which is capable of being revived in the present. Carlyle's book is remarkable not least for the vividness with which he recreates the life and imaginative world of this extremely remote society; even the great Lord Acton, a man who in general had little use for Carlyle, called it 'the most remarkable piece of historical thinking in the language'. As always, history is of value in Carlyle's eyes only if the historian can make it alive to the reader in the same sense as the present is alive. But what chiefly concerns him is that twelfth-century Bury St Edmund's is a society not yet infected by individualism, in which men are attached to each other by bonds other than cash, and, above all, men's instinct for recognising their superiors finds easy and natural outlet. The Abbey, at the beginning of the chronicle, is in a sad state of debt and dereliction, under the control of an incompetent abbot. After his death, the mode of electing a new abbot is apparently confused, illogical and arbitrary; but because the true instinct of hero-worship is there, the process produces the right man, the reforming Abbot Samson. As was the case with all Carlyle's heroes, Samson is anything but a Utopian. He is a hard-headed realist, a harsh disciplinarian, a sharp man of business, a man whose religion is for the most part inarticulate and instinctive, though wholly sincere. Implied throughout is the contrast with an England governed by a Parliament elected on approved Reform Bill principles, but which, because a society blinded by crass materialist individualism can no longer recognise its heroes, fails to throw up a government capable of coping with the social crisis of the day.

The other major novelty of *Past and Present* is its sharp categorisation of the upper classes of British society into 'Dilettantes' and 'Mammonists'. 'Dilettantes' are the privileged land-owning aristocracy, who, like the aristocracy of France before 1789, have abandoned the duties of governing and retained only its privileges, symbolised again by the Corn Laws and the Game Laws, becoming a class of idle and unproductive parasites; 'Mammonists' are the industrial middle class, whom Carlyle indeed vastly prefers to the Dilettantes because they do work (to the extent of transforming the entire face of England), but whom he also condemns because they work blindly, with no aim but the accumulation of wealth, lacking both a sense of the sacramental nature of work and an awareness of their moral responsibility for the well-being of their employees. England can be saved only by the emergence of a new, morally responsible, working aristocracy, a phenomenon he sees as much more likely to arise from the new middle classes than from the old aristocracy. His imagination was still fired by the vision of the Industrial Revolution as a grand creative achievement; Arkwright and Brindley are among his heroes. At the lower levels of society, the suffering mass of the working classes demand the relief to which they are fully entitled. But their physical hardships are secondary; what they stand in greatest need of is a sense of purpose and direction, a sense that though life may be hard there is a justice behind it. Above all their demand is for leadership, for heroes to rule them. In the end their demand will be met, for if the existing ruling class cannot mend its ways and show itself capable of heroism, Britain will follow France, and find its heroes through revolution.

This was Carlyle's message to his readers at the peak of his prophetic career. As a prophet must, he was saying what they felt needed to be said, but could not effectively articulate for themselves. What was it in Carlyle that struck the deepest echo in the intelligent and sensitive reader of the 1840s? Certainly not a programme of specific action, but something deeper and more resounding. There were three major elements in his message that were likely to have aroused most response: the assertion of an absolute and transcendent moral order, which made life a matter of urgent and unsparing moral challenge (*Past and Present* bore the Goethean epigraph 'Ernst ist das Leben' – 'Life is earnest' – on its title-page); the assertion of social responsibility, and the demand for a line of personal and governmental action which should embody it; and the claim that the truest revelation of the divine was history, and that history in the long run always works for justice. These assertions supported by far the most complete and balanced response to the phenomenon of the Industrial Revolution and industrial society that had yet been achieved, the first indeed to get it into any kind of proper perspective. This was Carlyle's finest achievement as a social critic, and it still commands respect. It was spontaneous, it was undogmatic, it felt with equal sensitivity and emphasised with equal force both the creative and inhuman aspects of the Industrial Revolution, it recognised it as a moral phenomenon demanding above all a moral and an active response. In *Chartism* and *Past and Present*, modern industrialism has some of the qualities of 'Sansculottism' in the later books of *The French Revolution* (though Carlyle never characterises it as clearly): it forces itself upon the observer like a monster risen from the deep – vast, morally ambivalent, at once divine and infernal, and demanding from him a response in whose making he passes judgement upon himself.

In expressing this vision of the new industrialised society, Carlyle gave voice to the anxieties and the hopes of the best minds of the generation of the 1840s; and in these authoritative statements, it seemed for a time possible for the religious and social anxieties of the generation to find satisfaction. Orthodox Christianity might no longer be possible, but a solid moral order, and even a sense of a divine transcendence, remained. Life had a purpose, and its fulfilment or non-fulfilment was a matter of critical importance for the eternal well-being of the individual concerned. That purpose could be fulfilled only in socially responsible work, and it demanded heroism. And though the revelation of the Scriptures and the authority of the Church could no longer be taken on faith, history was divine and just, and in such contemporary events as the rise of the Chartist movement, the affairs of Ireland, and the revolutions of 1848, the divine monition could be very clearly heard.

This was a strenuous, if inexact, moral creed. In a way which neither of the major religious movements of the age, Evangelicalism and the Oxford Movement, had contrived to do, it united the call to religious commitment with the call to social action, and in doing so it spoke to the deepest anxieties of that worried, radical, socially conscientious generation. The clearest evidence of this is the extent to which so much of the best-known and most influential social criticism of the age adopts Carlylean formulations. The brief flowering of the so-called 'social novel' in the late 1840s and early 1850s is a case in point. The mere appearance of the form, and the popular success of the books in question, is evidence enough of the state of the public mind at the time and its concern with social issues. More relevant here, though, is the extent to which almost all its leading examples show clear evidence of Carlyle's influence, whether this is demonstrable, as in the case of Mrs Gaskell's *Mary Barton* and *North and South*, Kingsley's *Yeast* and *Alton Locke*, and Dickens's *Hard Times*, or only presumable as in the case of Disraeli's *Sybil*. All these books proclaim, in Carlylean tones, the intolerable distress of the working man, the neglect of his betters, the necessity for a morally regenerated leadership. Gradgrind in *Hard Times* is exactly Carlyle's 'Mammonist': Mr Carson in *Mary Barton* and Mr Thornton in *North and South* are, by the end of the books, exactly the morally regenerated 'captains of industry' for whom Carlyle had called. Barnakill in *Yeast* and Sandy Mackaye in *Alton Locke* are even Carlyle himself. All these books reject, as Carlyle rejected, any purely political solution of the crisis, including Chartism. And all of them surely owed part of their successful appeal to their middle-class readership precisely to this fact, to their rejection of democracy and their ultimate conservatism. Indeed, Carlyle himself can be classed as a conservative, if the vehement rejection of democracy and a consistent and total lack of interest in the redistribution of wealth constitute conservatism. But the categorisation, if it is to be made, requires so many qualifications that it seems to lose most of its value. The social novelists all represent a watering-down of the more radical elements of Carlyle's thinking. They are all, for example (with the possible exception of Dickens), much concerned to demonstrate the continuing relevance of orthodox Christianity, which Carlyle denied. Not only so, but Carlyle was generally regarded as a radical in his lifetime, both by himself and by others; and

certainly conservatives of his own time showed themselves anything but eager to turn for help to this eccentric and dangerous
figure.

Carlyle belonged to the world of the literary intelligentsia,
and it is no surprise that it is there that it is easiest to trace his
influence. His contacts with the political world, other than with
the small group of radical MPs such as Charles Buller, were
occasional and slight. But even in this field the 1840s witnessed
a continuing concern with morally-inspired humanitarian social
reform that coincided closely with Carlyle's, if in a less radical
key, and that illustrated the aptness of his prophetic message to
the decade, even if the extent of Carlyle's contribution to it cannot be precisely defined. Obvious examples are the great public
campaign for the repeal of the Corn Laws orchestrated by the
Anti-Corn Law League, Ashley's campaigns for factory and
mines legislation, the relaxation of the administration of the
Poor Law under the continuing pressure of public opinion, the
campaign for public health legislation that finally found expression in the Public Health Act of 1848, and the increasing concern for public education. On a smaller scale, the Christian
Socialist movement founded by J. M. Ludlow and F. D.
Maurice in 1848, with the ready co-operation of Charles Kingsley, represents exactly Carlyle's combination of religious and
social concern, albeit in a more orthodox fashion. Humanitarian
social reform was as much the characteristic concern of British
politics in the 1840s as political reform in the 1830s or foreign
policy in the 1850s; and of this state of mind Carlyle, as its
prophet, was both producer and product.

Carlyle was keenly concerned, too, with the practical imple-
mentation of his ideas at this time, and with finding a leader to
undertake the task. His increasing public reputation did bring
him into contact at least with the fringe of the aristocratic political world in the later 1840s. He met and admired Cobden; but
more significantly, after Peel's repeal of the Corn Laws in 1846,
he came increasingly to see in Peel the one man with the conscience, the awareness of the need of the moment, and the ability, to undertake the regeneration of British politics and society.
Peel was the only British statesmen of Carlyle's lifetime in
whom he saw, if only briefly, the hope of heroic status; and

indeed some of Peel's thinking of the later 1840s does suggest a conception of social reform not wholly remote from Carlyle's ideas. Carlyle met Peel more than once, and after his fall in 1846 eagerly anticipated his return to office; he seems even to have hoped for official employment under him. But Peel's death in a riding accident in 1850 ended all these hopes, and Carlyle's never very strong expectations of any good coming out of the existing British political system died with him.

For all these striking points of resemblance between Carlyle's prophetic message and the public concerns of the 1840s, there is at least one striking point of divergence. At no point was Carlyle's insistence on the role of the hero convincingly echoed, even by a public opinion otherwise sympathetic to what he had to say. This difference was to grow wider and not narrower, and in the end was to destroy altogether the close communion between Carlyle and his public on which his role as prophet depended. Even if Carlyle's middle- and upper-class readers were comforted by his repudiation of democracy, the Chartist solution for the crisis, few of them were attracted by the markedly authoritarian strain in his teachings. Moreover, this strain in Carlyle became more emphatic as the decade went by. It was already dominant in 1840 in *Heroes and Hero-Worship*, but so far primarily in the fields of religion and literature. By the time he published *Past and Present* in 1843 the hero has become Samson, the practical reformer, and his hoped-for imitator in nineteenth-century England. In the same year appeared 'Dr Francia', a review article in which Carlyle conferred heroic status on a contemporary dictator of Paraguay; and from now on all Carlyle's heroes would be, not priests, prophets, or poets, but political despots. Increasingly the hero does not so much *enlighten* men as *compel* them.

The next great milestone along this road was the publication, in 1845, of the long-postponed history of the seventeenth-century Puritan Revolution, in the form, finally, of the *Letters and Speeches of Oliver Cromwell*. What started as a history of a popular movement, analogous to the French Revolution, ended up as a full-blooded eulogy of the Lord Protector. Carlyle originally conceived the *Letters and Speeches* as a mere preliminary to a biography of Cromwell, but eventually came to see them as a substitute. *Cromwell* is one of Carlyle's three major works of history, and it is undoubtedly a remarkable work in its own right. By it, as he had done in *The French Revolution*, Carlyle to a very large extent succeeded in reversing an entire tradition of historiography, and in this case one that had stood for nearly two centuries: the picture of Cromwell as a fanatical, hypocritical and ruthless political adventurer. Carlyle's Cromwell is a religious idealist, a man of wrestling and tormented sincerity; and from this interpretation the whole subsequent tradition of Cromwellian biography down to our own day descends. *Cromwell* is the only one of Carlyle's histories to have retained any strictly historical authority down to our own day, the only one that a modern professional historian would ever dream of consulting; though it owes this to its form, a collection of primary source material, and not at all to the fiercely subjective commentary which Carlyle wove into it. By the standards of the age Carlyle was an extremely conscientious editor, both in tracking down Cromwell's papers and in transcribing them accurately, and it is a tribute to him that in this respect his work has never been replaced. Nevertheless, for all the occasional splendours of Carlyle's own prose, it must be reckoned a dull book beside *The French Revolution*. This is primarily because it has far less imaginative power. The sense of multiple levels of meaning, whether explicit or implicit, which perpetually haunts the reader of that masterpiece, is wholly absent here. There is none of the earlier use of symbols, nothing like the plastic sense of blind unconscious forces working through history and the conscious purposes of men that so informs Carlyle's account of the Terror; and though Carlyle certainly intended *Cromwell* to have contemporary reference and to carry a message of admonition to his readers, this quite fails to carry conviction here. Carlyle envisaged it as a kind of Book II of *Past and Present* on the grand scale, a new example of religiously-inspired heroic action from the past to point the need for it in the present; but even in *Past and Present* the analogy between twelfth-century Bury St Edmund's and nineteenth-century England is too remote to be convincing. In *Cromwell* the analogy is left implicit for the most part, and few of its readers then or since can have taken much notice of it. The book also has its embarrassments for the Carlylean: the fiercely enthusiastic interjections with which Carlyle punctuates Cromwell's speeches and, much more seriously, the overt and emphatic approval which he bestows, not merely on Cromwell's high-handed methods with Parliaments, but also on the grisly massacres which followed the capture of Drogheda and Wexford, during his suppression of the Irish revolt.

Carlyle presented these as examples of providential chastisement of a wilfully rebellious people, an interpretation which was too strong for the stomachs of many even of his admirers, and which comes strangely from a man who had spoken so forthrightly of English injustice toward Ireland in *Chartism*, and who was indeed a personal friend of some of the leaders of the nationalist 'Young Ireland' movement of his own day. It is another example of how Carlyle's increasing emphasis on the actions of the God-given hero in the role of political despot was beginning to open a gap between him and his disciples in the later 1840s. His old friend Emerson, revisiting England in 1847 for the first time since the Carlyles' Craigenputtock days, saw the difference in him. 'Carlyle', Emerson remarked, 'is no idealist in opinions, but a protectionist in political economy, aristocratic in politics, epicene in diet, goes for murder, money, punishment by death, slavery, and all the pretty abominations, tempering them with epigrams.' The fact that the friendship between the two men remained unbroken only strengthens the judgement.

# 6 The decline of the prophet

Carlyle's evolving opinions were treading hard on the toes of his former liberal admirers by the late 1840s. In 1850 the publication of *Latter-Day Pamphlets* was to break the connection between them completely. The tone for these was sufficiently set by the appearance in a periodical the previous year of his 'Occasional Discourse on the Nigger Question', a denunciation of the Arcadian idleness in which the emancipated slaves of the British West Indies were reputed to be living, coupled with a demand that the universal moral obligation of work should be reimposed on them by a virtual restoration of slavery and the 'beneficent whip'. Of all Carlyle's writings, the 'Occasional Discourse' is the one that best retains its radicalism, if that can be defined by the capacity to create instant and intransigent hostility in almost all its readers. It stamps as hard on the moral shibboleths of the 1980s as it did, and was meant to do, on those of the age of anti-slavery idealism. It offended every shade of respectable opinion in Britain. It is true that Carlyle makes it clear that his defence of slavery, if such it was, was restricted to a heavily modified slavery with ample protection for the slave, even including his right to buy his own emancipation; but it seems likely that by this he merely forfeited his chance of winning the support of the one group that might have been expected to welcome the 'Discourse', the slave-owners of the American South, without conciliating any sizeable section of opinion at home. It is so hard to be just to the 'Occasional Discourse' that it does need emphasising that it takes its rise, however perversely, from something as seemingly blameless as Carlyle's idealisation of work; its central theme is identical with the proposal for 'permanence of contract' that had appeared in *Past and Present*, and it is not *primarily* a racist document. But racist it is nevertheless. It seems impossible to imagine any grounds on which to defend the contemptuous and brutal sarcasm of such passages as 'Our beautiful Black darlings are at last happy; with little labour except to the teeth, which surely, in those excellent horse-jaws of theirs, will not fail!' (E IV 350).

The *Latter-Day Pamphlets*, which followed in the first part of the succeeding year, keep the same tone, though they do not return to the same subject. They are a violent repudiation of liberalism and democracy alike in all their forms, an explosion of disgust at what Carlyle identifies as all the leading tendencies of the age: its constitutionalism, its cant, its materialism, its godlessness, its worship of sham heroes (typified by George Hudson, the 'Railway King', an unscrupulous company promoter), and its inability to find or recognise real ones. It is this inability which provides the nearest approach to a unifying theme running throughout the eight pamphlets, and by this time it was of course a familiar Carlylean text. There are constructive aspects to the *Pamphlets*, as in their insistence on the need for the strengthening of the administration at the expense of the legislature, the creation of non-elective seats in Parliament for permanent administrators, and the expansion of the sphere of government action at the expense of the ruling ideology of *laissez-faire*. But the general effect is overwhelmingly, very powerfully, and almost nihilistically negative. It is hard to think of any other equally forceful expression of generalised disgust at society in English except the writings of Swift. Sometimes the *Pamphlets* rise to savagely effective satire, as in the denunciation of utilitarianism in the guise of the 'Pig Philosophy' of the final pamphlet:

> Pig Propositions, in a rough form, are somewhat as follows: 1. The Universe, so far as sane conjecture can go, is an immeasurable Swine's-trough, consisting of solid and liquid, and of other contrasts and kinds; – especially consisting of attainable and unattainable, the latter in immensely greater quantity for most pigs. 2. Moral evil is unattainability of Pig's-wash; moral good, attainability of ditto . . . (D 316)

Another example is the endearing suggestion that some public figures might be more fittingly commemorated by a coalshaft than by a statue. But in general the disgust they express is too universal for this. The *Pamphlets* are the work of a man who is turning his back on the world in despair. If the role of the prophet is symbiotic, the man who wrote them was no longer a prophet, for he speaks from a position of self-conscious isolation. The prophetic parallel that comes to mind is that of Jonah sitting outside the redeemed city of Nineveh and complaining bitterly to the Almighty at the disappointment of his expectation that it would be destroyed. But the parallel does not extend far, for to the Carlyle of the *Latter-Day Pamphlets* the doom-clouds are still gathering blacker and blacker over the society of nineteenth-century Britain. His disgust at everything it stands for is validated by the imminent prospect of its apocalypse.

The appearance of *Latter-Day Pamphlets* marked the point of final alienation between Carlyle and every significant shade of liberal and radical opinion in mid-nineteenth-century Britain. Regarded with alarm by respectable conservatives as a dangerous radical, he was henceforth damned in the eyes of liberals and radicals as a reactionary and an admirer of despotism – a reputation that was only to be strengthened a decade later by the appearance of his last major work, the *History of Frederick the Great*. This is not to say that with the appearance of the *Pamphlets* Carlyle ceased to be a major figure on the British intellectual and literary scene. However violently readers might dissent from the opinions expressed in them, it was impossible to deny their force or the strength and originality of the mind that produced them. Carlyle lived another thirty years as the grand old *enfant terrible* of the English intellectual Establishment. But although his reputation survived, his prophetic function did not: he had lost the ear of the rising generation, and the last thirty years of his life were spent in an intellectual isolation almost as complete as that of his first forty.

Many factors converge in explanation of this growing isolation. A major change in the public mood was taking place in Britain between 1848 and 1851. The introverted doubt and social self-questioning that had characterised the 1840s was giving way to the mood of bellicose national self-confidence that typified the 1850s and was exemplified by Palmerston. One main reason for this change was Britain's successful survival of the period of the 1848 revolutions. Nearly every other state in Europe was shaken, but the established order in Britain, with the middle classes now safely recruited in its defence, rode the waves of the last great Chartist upsurge with triumphant ease. Another was the revival of trade after 1848, which made the 1850s a period of prosperity and widespread improvement in living standards. The new industrial society in Britain seemed to have survived its teething troubles, and to have emerged as a triumphant success. The mood of euphoria was perfectly mirrored in the success of the Great Exhibition in the summer of 1851, which was widely interpreted as a festival of renewed social harmony as well as of the marvels of the new technology.

This was a new generation, with which Carlyle was wholly out of sympathy. Britain's exemption from revolution in 1848 was no cause of triumph for him. His attitude to the continental revolutions of that year was a mixture of satisfaction at the destruction of what he had long denounced as the rotten shams of the existing political and social order, and of horror at the pit of democratic anarchy into which Europe appeared to be descending – he could detect in the revolutions no trace of the renewed sense of providential order and of recognition of true heroes which any hopeful regeneration of society must in his eyes have entailed. A revolution in Britain would at least have justified the warnings of divine judgement impending that had been a constant theme of all his public utterances since the publication of *The French Revolution*; and for a brief time in the spring there seemed to be a real threat of such a revolution, as alarm spread in London at the prospect of the gigantic Chartist demonstration planned for 10 April on Kennington Common. But Mammonists and Dilettantes alike rose in their might; 150,000 special constables were sworn in, and the demonstration collapsed in fiasco. Carlyle himself, on the morning of 10 April, walked into town to observe events. He got as far as the Burlington Arcade, when it came on to rain, and he returned home in a Chelsea omnibus. Despite its element of farce, there is also an element of symbolism in the incident. From this point onward, the course of current events would cease, at least in the eyes of most contemporary observers, to validate Carlyle's prophecies, and it may have been a recognition of the divergence that underlay the increasing stridency of the prophecies themselves. To most observers of the early 1850s things were not getting worse, they were manifestly getting better, even for the poorest. The sense of social crisis subsided. The values of the 1830s so mercilessly attacked by Carlyle and exposed to so much radical questioning in the 1840s, such as middle-class parliamentarianism and free trade economics, seemed to be triumphantly justified by the new turn of events. The apotheosis of this frame of mind was the Great Exhibition. Carlyle, logically enough, abominated it as the crowning expression of the crass materialistic optimism that he so abhorred (though he was still capable of responding with excitement to the technical novelty and daring of the Exhibition building, the Crystal Palace, itself).

One cause, then, of the decline in Carlyle's influence after the middle of the century was the abrupt shift in public mood in Britain, and the fact that events apparently ceased to bear him out. But as a complete explanation this is inadequate, because the divergence between Carlyle and his leading disciples can be traced back before 1848 – before events had turned against him, and before the public mood had discernibly changed. It was in 1848 itself that Arthur Hugh Clough, that type-figure of his generation, made one of the most significant comments ever made, both on Carlyle's exercise of the prophetic role, and on his forfeiture of it: 'Carlyle has led us out into the desert – and has left us there.' In accounting for this divergence, the point of departure must be Carlyle's growing emphasis on the role of the hero, which had been a point of difference between him and the bulk of his disciples from the start. The eager, intelligent, idealistic young men who looked to Carlyle as their guide in a time of troubles would probably have accepted democracy if he had demanded it of them. They would not accept despotism as the solution to the problems of the age. But a prophet's function is the memorable utterance of the unformed convictions of his hearers. How, in this instance, did Carlyle come to go so far astray in his interpretation of the role that in the end he forfeited their discipleship altogether?

Carlyle himself would have defined the role differently. Truth to him was a monition from on high, not something intuited from the subconscious minds of his listeners. But there was a progressive coarsening in the fibre of Carlyle's thinking and writing from the early 1840s onward, which has often been recognised by his critics but never completely analysed or diagnosed. Compare a passage from *Sartor Resartus* with one from *Past and Present*:

What, speaking in quite unofficial language, is the net-purport and upshot of war? To my own knowledge, for example, there dwell and toil, in the British village of Dumdrudge, usually some five-hundred souls. From these ... there are successively selected, during the French war, say thirty able-bodied men: Dumdrudge, at her own expense, has suckled and nursed them: she has, not without difficulty and sorrow, fed them up to manhood, and even trained them to crafts, so that one can weave, another build, another hammer, and the weakest can stand under thirty stone avoirdupois. Nevertheless, amid much weeping and swearing, they are selected; all dressed in red; and shipped away, at the public charges, some two-thousand miles, or say only to the south of Spain; and fed there till wanted. And now to that same spot, in the south of Spain, are thirty similar French artisans, from a French Dumdrudge, in like manner wending: till at length, after infinite effort, the two parties come into actual juxtaposition; and Thirty stands fronting Thirty, each with a gun in his hand. Straightway the word 'Fire!' is given: and they blow the souls out of one another; and in place of sixty brisk useful craftsmen, the world has sixty dead carcasses, which it must bury, and anew shed tears for. Had these men any quarrel? Busy as the Devil is, not the smallest! They lived far enough apart; were the entirest strangers; nay, in so wide a Universe, there was even, unconsciously, by Commerce, some mutual helpfulness between them. How then? Simpleton! their Governors had fallen out; and, instead of shooting one another, had the cunning to make these poor blockheads shoot. (S 139–40)

Who can despair of Governments that passes a Soldiers' Guardhouse, or meets a redcoated man on the streets! That a body of men could be got together to kill other men when you bade them: this, *a priori*, does it not seem one of the impossiblest things? Yet look, behold it: in the stolidest of Donothing Governments, that impossibility is a thing done ...

It is incalculable what, by arranging, commanding and regi-
menting, you can make of men. These thousand straight-
standing firmest individuals, who shoulder arms, who march,
wheel, advance, retreat; and are, for your behoof, a magazine
charged with fiery death, in the most perfect condition of
potential activity: few months ago, till the persuasive sergeant
came, what were they? Multiform ragged losels, runaway
apprentices, starved weavers, thievish valets; an entirely
broken population, fast tending towards the treadmill. But
the persuasive sergeant came; by tap of drum enlisted, or
formed lists of them, took heartily to drilling them; – and he
and you have made them this! (P 260, 262)

The loss of humanity between these passages is surely unquestionable. In *Sartor*, he starts with the men, innocent craftsmen and members of a healthy little community, and sees the
fate that comes upon them as a brutal injustice. In *Past and
Present* they are already soldiers when we meet them, and it is
only as soldiers drilled to the mechanical perfection of robots
that they are admirable. In their previous lives they have been
nothing but 'ragged losels, runaway apprentices, starved weavers, thievish valets'. This may be an accurate observation of the
levels of society from which the British Army recruited its rank
and file in the 1840s; but the change in attitude to the mass of
mankind is sadly typical of the later Carlyle, the Carlyle of the
'Occasional Discourse' who can wax sarcastic about 'our beautiful Black darlings' of the West Indies, and of the *Latter-Day
Pamphlets*, with its dismissal of his fellow-countrymen as 'twenty-
seven millions mostly fools'. This is a note wholly missing in
his work of the 1830s, and only just becoming audible in *Past
and Present* in 1843; for beside the passage just quoted, with its
message of the worthlessness of undrilled humanity, have to be
set passages like the deeply humane description of the paupers
in the St Ives workhouse at the beginning of the book. But after
*Past and Present* that note is never clearly heard again. Ordinary
men and women are no longer the simple, long-suffering,
much-abused folk of *The French Revolution* and *Chartism* who
require no more than rulers conscious of their responsibility before God whom they can readily follow and admire; instead they

are idle, greedy, shiftless wastrels, redeemable only by the serf's collar, the slave-driver's whip, the iron and merciless discipline of Frederick the Great's drill-sergeants. The transition is masked, so effectively that it has often gone unobserved, by the continuity of the theme of hero-worship; but the content of this theme itself undergoes a great change between the 1830s, when the hero is the poet like Burns, the religious reformer like Knox, or the revolutionary leader like Mirabeau – divinely inspired, risen from the depths, charismatic, instinctively recognised – and the 1840s and 1850s, when he is the dictator like Francia, the military despot like Cromwell, even the absolutist hereditary monarch like Frederick the Great, whose heroism is imposed, not spontaneously recognised, and imposed primarily by superior military force.

The paradox of all this is that Carlyle was by nature a deeply humane man, and when he met hardship and poverty in the flesh his reactions, to the end of his life, were instinctively and touchingly generous and sympathetic. But in the change in his attitude to men in the mass, and in his interpretation of the nature of the hero, we are close to the secret of how at the end of the 1840s he came to lose his hold on his disciples; and the origin of these changes must be found in the recesses of his remarkable personality. That personality had always been subject to enormous internal pressures. Carlyle's real greatness, perhaps, lay in the ability to endure greater internal stresses and to hold them in balance for longer than any ordinary man. Some of these stresses may have been sexual. Some were certainly physical, such as the sleeplessness and dyspepsia that tormented him all his life. In addition he had a nervous system pathologically sensitive to the impacts of the outside world, a characteristic which appears equally in his horror of noise, in the marvellous vividness of his powers of description, and in his intensely humane response to the spectacle of human suffering. 'Such *skinless* creatures' was his very apt description of himself and his wife. But this sensitivity could easily become unendurable. Because he felt so powerfully, he dared not feel very often. Because of this, there was a constant urge in Carlyle to cut himself off from the world altogether – to retire to Craigenputtock, to emigrate to America, to build the famous 'soundproof room' for himself in Cheyne Row. The loss of humanity in his later writings is to some extent the sign of a natural tenderness so battered by the pains of the world that in the end it takes refuge in brutality, in refusing to feel at all.

But this is not the whole story. There is also apparent in the later Carlyle an increasing rejection of the spontaneous and the instinctive, even the creative, in favour of the imposed, the authoritarian and the repressive, and this must also have originated in his personality. Carlyle was aware of enormous forces within himself, forces of which he only partly approved, which he partly feared, and which he could only very imperfectly control. It is, surely, from them that the idea of 'Sansculottism' in *The French Revolution* derives its dynamic and deeply ambivalent significance. As this example shows, Carlyle in his prime was able to allow these forces expression, to admit them at least partially to his conscious mind, and so tap the enormously powerful creativity that appears unforgettably in *Sartor* and *The French Revolution*. But he was like a man on the nozzle of an immensely powerful fire-hose. The strain involved was tremendous, and by the 1840s the temptation to turn it off, to shut down the powerful and destructive forces of instinct once and for all, was becoming irresistible. The elevation of the role of the military despot in his later works is the intellectual reflection of this; and because it was essentially a response to a private need, it awoke no echo in, and finally alienated, most of his disciples. The critic G. C. Le Roy suggested that the mob, in all Carlyle's writings, is the equivalent of his instincts, and this seems to me entirely right. The shifting tensions within his personality are mirrored in his changing attitude to the mass of ordinary men and women. As long as he can accept his instincts, they are at least partly benign. When he felt driven to wall them off, his capacity for sympathy with the many atrophied. It is this that accounts for the apparent loss of creativity in the later writings, and for the disappearance of the sense of overlapping levels of meaning which makes *Sartor* and *The French Revolution* such exciting books to read. A single despotic level of Carlyle's personality has usurped authority over his mind. The fruitful tensions have gone – the tensions which, for instance, had enabled him to see simultaneously and with equal vividness both the creative and the destructive aspects of the Industrial Revolution, or of the New Poor Law in *Chartism*. A single value judgement, and a single point of view, now dominate all.

It was because of these shifts in his personality that Carlyle was unable to see anything more than sheer destructiveness and blank anarchy in the revolutions of 1848, an attitude so strikingly less complex and instructive than his interpretation of the French Revolution of 1789 eleven years earlier; and it was precisely this sort of failure that drove a wedge between him and his disciples, most of whom (like Clough) probably instinctively sympathised with the rebels. They would have accepted a call to revolution from Carlyle, but not a call to despotism, and it is possible now to see why Carlyle's way began to diverge from theirs at this point.

An element of personal frustration on a more superficial level may also have played some part in driving Carlyle into isolation at this time. Humility and self-doubt were qualities that had their place in Carlyle's complex personality; but he was a proud man. He was well aware, as no able man can well fail to be, of his own intellectual superiority to the vast majority of those around him, whose neglect and contempt he had nevertheless had to endure for years. Even more, he was burningly conscious of having a message of the most crucial importance to communicate to them, which most of them refused to hear. It would be naïve to assume that Carlyle's constant recurrence to the theme of hero-worship had no reference to his conception of his own position in society. He cannot have failed to see himself as the heroic prophet sent by heaven to lead the British people back to the sincerity, the sense of duty and divine purpose they had lost since the days of Oliver Cromwell. The identification once made, it stares out at the reader inescapably from passage after passage of *Past and Present* and *Latter-Day Pamphlets*. The point is strengthened by Carlyle's repeatedly expressed yearnings in the 1840s to get away from literature to play a part in the practical work of cleansing the Augean stables, preferably by taking an official post. But the possibility, which had seemed so strong in the earlier part of the decade, that the British public might indeed hear his word and take it to heart receded. After

1848, history itself seemed to turn against him. Events no longer seemed to justify his prognosis of imminent doom for contemporary society (a fact, incidentally, which was causing Karl
Marx some not dissimilar problems at the same time). Peel, on
whom he had pinned his hopes both for the reform of Britain
and Ireland and for his own employment in the work, was kill-
ed in a riding accident. It is not so surprising, then, if Carlyle's
mind turned increasingly to the idea of finding a shorter way
than persuasion and conversion to bend men to his ends, if he
was attracted increasingly by the illusion that the despot could
succeed where the prophet had failed, and that though the mass
of men were too far sunk in beer and balderdash to hear his
message, the rod and the whip might yet coerce them into salvation. But this was a road on which few or none of his disciples
would follow him. To transform his message in this way was to
lose the vital communion with the young, the eager and the
intelligent on which his very role as prophet depended.

The final phase of Carlyle's intellectual development is
summed up monumentally in his *History of Frederick the Great*,
the last and most laborious of all his books, whose writing occupied him for no less than thirteen years, from 1852 to 1865.
Before he started work on it, Carlyle also wrote another, much
briefer and much more attractive book, the *Life of John Sterling*. Sterling was not Carlyle's hero but his friend, and the book
reveals better than any of his other writings the warmth, the
open-heartedness, and the sympathetic insight into character
that made so many of his contemporaries value Carlyle's
friendship so highly. For once, the prophetic mantle is laid by.
The *Life* is also an important document for the moral and intellectual history of Sterling's generation, exactly the generation
among whom Carlyle recruited his most enthusiastic disciples.
Together with the posthumous *Reminiscences* it is probably the
most easily approachable (though certainly not the most easily
obtainable) of all Carlyle's books, and placed as it is between
the uncompromising harshness of the *Latter-Day Pamphlets* and
the *History of Frederick the Great*, it is a timely reminder of the
profound humanity that existed in Carlyle beneath all the apparent inhumanity.

*Frederick* itself adds nothing of importance to the ideas

already expressed in *Oliver Cromwell* and the *Latter-Day Pamphlets*. By the time he set about it, Carlyle was already approaching sixty, and by the time it was finished he was nearly seventy. It is therefore a work of his old age, and lacks the creativity and the intellectual suppleness of his early writings. It cost him even more agonies than any of his other works. It involved him, to whom journeys and sleeping away from home were always major ordeals, in two considerable visits to Germany. There were the usual battles with inadequate sources: and, all in all, it is a tribute to his dogged sense of dedication that the book was ever completed. Its tone is both authoritarian and didactic. It is without the many-sidedness and dazzling imaginative force of *The French Revolution*. It is weighed down by an immense mass of narrative detail, and by a hero-figure whom even its author could not completely admire and whose cynical political realism most of its English readers, at any rate, have found thoroughly unattractive. It is by far the least-read of Carlyle's major works, and there seems small reason to expect any increase in its popularity in the future. Yet *Frederick* has remarkable qualities. The rise of Prussia and the Hohenzollern dynasty is traced not only in great detail, but with great fidelity and great clarity. These, perhaps, are basic qualifications in any historian; more surprising are the gusto and frequent humour with which it is written, which certainly would not suggest an ageing author to any unknowing reader, and the vividness of the character-drawing, the topography, and especially the battle pieces which form the high points of the narrative.

The choice of a foreign subject is always something which requires explanation in a historian, but in Carlyle's case it can be seen as the natural culmination of several tendencies in his life, especially, of course, his long-standing enthusiasm for German literature and German thought, but also his increasingly authoritarian idea of hero-worship, and his abiding interest in the eighteenth century as the origin of the intellectual environment which had shaped his youth and the direction of his own ideas. Frederick the Great is 'the last of the Kings', the last authentically heroic national leader in European history, before the pervasive scepticism, democracy and anarchy of the nineteenth century made any such figure unthinkable. He had to work in an environment already polluted by the rationalism of the Enlightenment, and it is in that fact that Carlyle finds the excuse for his limitations, above all his complete lack of the religious earnestness that Carlyle had previously demanded of his heroes. His heroism lies essentially in his realism and his freedom from the cant that Carlyle saw as so typical of the Enlightenment. This respect for hard fact is the nearest approximation to the sense of the divine working in history that the eighteenth century was capable of; and in Frederick's case it is demonstrated above all by the success of his military coup in seizing Silesia from the ailing Hapsburg Empire, and in retaining it in the face of the united military effort of most of Europe. In *Frederick* the judgement of Providence has become identical with military success: might has indeed become right. It is clear that Carlyle himself is unhappy with this conclusion, from the uncomfortable contortions of his attempts to demonstrate the justice of Frederick's claims to Silesia; but the concentration of the narrative on the two great wars of Frederick's reign, the War of the Austrian Succession and the Seven Years War, and the dominance of the battle pieces, leave little room for doubt on the issue.

There are other things of interest in the book: the anticipation of later nineteenth-century imperialism in Carlyle's picture of Britain pursuing the imperial mission dictated to it by Providence, blindly except for the brief interlude of clear-sighted leadership under the elder Pitt, and the consistent juxtaposing of a pious, grave, moral, Protestant Prussia against a sceptical, frivolous, immoral, Catholic France – a pair of stereotypes which Carlyle projected into the history of his own time, and which a few years later he exultantly saw justified in the outcome of the Franco-Prussian War. There are plenty of incidental pleasures to be had from a reading of *Frederick the Great*; but the implausibility of the claims it makes on behalf of its central figure, and the one-dimensional quality of its writing as contrasted with Carlyle's earlier books, are flaws which rule out any serious claim to include it among his major achievements.

Nevertheless, it was recognised in its time as the final consolidation of Carlyle's literary achievement. It was strikingly symbolised from Germany itself by the award to him of the

Prussian Order of Merit in 1874; and indeed the last thirty years of Carlyle's life were in many respects years of triumph. He was offered the Order of the Bath by Disraeli, but refused it. He was elected Rector of Edinburgh University, and delivered a hugely successful inaugural address. But although his position in the literary establishment was unassailable and unique, it was, as he well knew, the position no longer of the prophet but of the sage. The distinction is vital: the prophet emerges from the desert to speak words of life to his people; the sage dwells remote upon his mountain-top, awe-inspiring but unapproached. He never recovered the ear of the public, and indeed alienated further much of that part of it which had once looked to him as mentor by his contemptuous dismissal of the Northern cause in the American Civil War and his vituperative denunciation of the Second Reform Act in Britain. His alienation from his own times became more and time complete; and in terms of ideas, his writings after 1850, considerable though they were in bulk, added nothing of significance to the position he had reached by the end of the 1840s. After 1865 he published no more books, though he left behind him for posthumous publication the marvellously vivid and wistful *Reminiscences* and the *Letters and Papers* of his wife, whose death in 1866 was a blow from which he never completely recovered. His own death in 1881 came as a long-awaited release. In accordance with his own wishes and his lifelong contempt for all forms of public pomp, the offer of burial in Westminster Abbey was declined, and he was buried beside his family in the churchyard of Ecclefechan.

# 7 Epilogue

The question whether Carlyle was a great man is both easy and hard to answer. Few men have been more unanimously recognised as great by their contemporaries and by those who knew them. But if one is asked to define the nature of that greatness exactly, the difficulties soon appear. Compared with thinkers like Burke and Marx, Carlyle has added nothing to the permanent stock of the world's ideas. The problem is compounded by the fact that, in the last hundred years, the world has not gone his way. Carlyle's notion of radicalism, which rested on a transformation of human relationships based on a fundamentally religious understanding of man's place in the universe, may be potentially the most fruitful one; but, in twentieth-century terms, it was a radicalism of the right, and that radicalism, disfigured by its own twentieth-century excesses, has lost out in practice to the rival radicalism of the left, based on the pursuit of egalitarianism and the transfer of political power. One is back with the familiar question of whether it is worth arguing with the course of history (especially given Carlyle's own propensity to regard history as the final court of appeal). Maybe the same is true of his historiography: perhaps Carlyle's notion of the function of history, with its emphasis on total imaginative recreation and the interpretation of the past as a record of the relationship of human societies with the transcendent justice (or is it the transcendent reality?) that overrules them, was a similar blind alley, which all later historiography has resolutely and wisely rejected. But this can be granted only with the major reservation that *The French Revolution*, at least, showed that this kind of history *could* be written, and written wonderfully.

If Carlyle was neither philosopher, political thinker, social theorist or historian of the first order, what was he? He was an important transmitter of the ideas of the late eighteenth-century German intellectual revolution to Britain; but others share this distinction, and it could hardly be made the basis of a claim to greatness. He was the author of two great masterpieces of the literary imagination, *Sartor Resartus* and *The French Revolution*; recent academic interest in Carlyle has been largely confined to critics and literary scholars, and it is as a literary figure that Carlyle's contemporary reputation stands highest. It is, though, ironic if this is to be the basis of Carlyle's claim to greatness, for there are few roles for himself that Carlyle would have repudiated more vehemently than that of the artist. He abhorred the notion of art, literary or otherwise, as an end in itself. The one acceptable role for the writer of his own luckless generation, he repeatedly insisted, was as prophet. As he said in the passage already quoted from one of his early letters to Mill, 'Not in Poetry, but only if so might be in Prophecy, in stern old-Hebrew denunciation, can one speak of the accursed realities that now, and for generations...weigh heavy on us!' (T VI 370). He was not interested in writing for posterity: he wanted to deliver a message to his own generation. Perhaps the most penetrating nineteenth-century judgement of Carlyle's importance was made by George Eliot as early as 1855, and it carries more weight because she could never be classed as one of his disciples, but at most as his detached and discriminating admirer:

> It is an idle question to ask whether his books will be read a century hence; if they were all burnt as the grandest of Suttees on his funeral pile, it would be only like cutting down an oak after its acorns have sown a forest. For there is hardly a superior or active mind of this generation that has not been modified by Carlyle's writings; there has hardly been an English book written for the last ten or twelve years that would not have been different if Carlyle had not lived.

The true nature of Carlyle's greatness is missed if one insists on looking for *enduring* memorials of it, even though those memorials may in fact exist (the books *are* still read; Carlyle *is* often recognised as one of the major originators of a tradition of moral criticism of industrial society that persists vigorously to the present day). Carlyle never saw himself as an artist, or an original thinker. He aspired to be a prophet, a man with a message for his age, and for one brief decade he fulfilled that role. It is not every generation that needs, or deserves, a prophet,

and those that need one do not always find one; but the generation of the 1840s was lucky. In Carlyle they found the greatest
example of the type in modern times, a man who could express
memorably the anxieties and the aspirations they felt, but were
only half aware of, or could not themselves articulate. Carlyle
fulfilled this role for a bare decade, in a lifetime of eighty years,
and even for this decade his success was incomplete. He never
succeeded in producing a programme of practical action in sufficiently concrete terms (a notion which he himself would have
dismissed as a mere formula, and hence an illusion; but is this
more than an escape?); and before long, the pursuit of his own
private compulsions drove him away tangentially from the best
minds of the generation that had revered him. There is pathos
in recalling the passage on Mirabeau from *The French Revolution* in which the half-conscious identification with Carlyle himself occurs: 'like a burning mountain he blazes heaven-high;
and, for twenty-three resplendent months, pours out, in flame
and molten fire-torrents, all that is in him, the Pharos and Won-
der-sign of an amazed Europe; – and then lies hollow, cold for
ever!' Carlyle's time of greatness was longer than Mirabeau's,
but still short enough; for prophets are ephemeral creatures by
the nature of their calling. Carlyle's achievement is local in both
time and place. He is neither a philosopher, nor a major figure
of European, as distinct from British, intellectual history.
Nevertheless, in the years between 1837 and 1848 his social criticism was characterised by an immensely fruitful tension, between the moral and the practical, between marvel and horror
at the achievements and monstrosities of industrialism, that was
equalled by no other critic of the nineteenth century, and by an
inconsistent but nevertheless profound humanity that enabled
him to function as the voice and the conscience of the most
open and socially sensitive generation of the nineteenth century.

# Further reading

## Carlyle's works

The standard edition of Carlyle's collected works is the Centenary Edition (London, 1896–9). It is less than satisfactory, especially because it is incomplete; it omits, notably, the *Reminiscences*. A new and fuller collected edition is at present projected. All the major works, other than the *Life of John Sterling* and the *History of Frederick the Great*, are also available in Everyman Library editions. Two good modern annotated editions (both American, like so much Carlyle scholarship) are C. F. Harrold's *Sartor Resartus* (1937) and Richard Altick's *Past and Present* (1977). A convenient introductory selection is the Penguin *Thomas Carlyle: Selected Writings* of 1971. It would be unthinkable not to refer also to the collected edition of Carlyle's and his wife's letters being published jointly by Duke and Edinburgh Universities, under the editorship of C. R Sanders and K. J. Fielding (1970) – the nine volumes so far published reach to 1837. Thomas and Jane were both letter-writers of genius, and the publication of this meticulous edition is far more than a merely scholarly event.

## Biographies

J. A. Froude's four-volume biography of 1882–4 has dominated this field, by attraction or repulsion, ever since it was written, and still stands as one of the great milestones of Victorian official biography, and as a major work of art in its own right; there is a very useful recent annotated one-volume abridgement edited by John Clubbe (London, 1979). Froude's book is a work of strong character, and has been subjected to fierce criticism, much of it justified, ever since it was written; but it has never been superseded. Of numerous one-volume biographies, the most recent and best-informed is Ian Campbell's *Thomas Carlyle* (London, 1974); unlike Froude, it is strongest on the Scottish period of Carlyle's life. The time is rapidly becoming ripe for a major new biography, especially now that the letters are being published. Thea Holme's *The Carlyles at Home* (London, 1965) is a most entertaining account of the Carlyles' idiosyncratic domestic life in London.

## Criticism

The bulk of critical writing about Carlyle is enormous. Much of the best of it is American, and on the whole literary in its orientation. Two major landmarks are C. F. Harrold's *Carlyle and German Thought* (Yale, 1934) and G. B. Tennyson's *Sartor Called Resartus* (Princeton, 1965). Invidious though it is to single out items in this vast field, I must also mention A. J. La-Valley's *Carlyle and the Idea of the Modern* (1968) – the most original and illuminating recent interpretation of Carlyle that I have read. Easier of access than these books to most English readers is Raymond Williams's interesting treatment of Carlyle in *Culture and Society, 1780–1950* (London, 1958). Those seeking further guidance should turn to G. B. Tennyson's superb discursive bibliography of Carlyle in *Victorian Prose: a Guide to Research*, edited by David J. DeLaura and published by the Modern Language Association of America (New York, 1973).

# Index